# PRAISE FOR DAVID HOULE

## The Shift Age

"*The Shift Age* lifts us out of the rapids of techno-change and helps us see the course of the river we've been rafting in."

–**Howard Bloom**, Author of *The God Problem: How a Godless Cosmos Creates* and *Global Brain: The Evolutions of Mass Mind from the Big Bang to the 21ˢᵗ Century*

"An enlightening view of the muck and miracle of it all. I highly recommend this eye-opening book."

–**Susan Jeffers**, Ph.D., Author of *Feel the Fear and Do it Anyway*

"Fills a useful niche between the technical emphasis of Kurzweil and the societal aspects of Toffler."

–**Dennis Bushnell**, Scientist

"David Houle's *Shift Age* offers an astounding proposition: the Information Age is ending with emergence of an age of constant change. Read this book!"

–**Reese Schonfeld**, Cofounder of CNN, CNN Headline News, and Food Network

"*The Shift Age* is a well-written and pivotal book by a sharp-eyed futurist with a gift for being ahead of the curve."

–**Richard Noyes**, Former Associate Director of the Center for Advanced Engineering Study at the Massachusetts Institute of Technology

"Every aspect of our lives is being impacted by the rapid and radical acceleration of technological change. David Houle's important book *The Shift Age* is a fascinating navigational tool that will help guide you as you speed into a future than even our imagination cannot adequately prepare us to steer through."

–**Jack Myers**, Editor and Publisher of www.JackMyers.com

"Capturing the dynamics, distress, and decisions we all face, *The Shift Age* is the travel guide for the future"

–**Tom Hudson**, *Nightly Business Report* Anchor

*Shift Ed: A Call to Action for the Transformation of K–12 Education*
"America needs a new educational vision. *Shift Ed* provides a clear vision that emphasized the essential ingredients of a twenty-first-century education based upon creativity, collaboration, and critical thinking. Houle makes a great case that nothing less than transformation will be enough."

–**Daniel Pink**, Author of *A Whole New Mind* and *Drive*

"We can't educate the leaders of tomorrow with yesterday's education model. Houle offers a much needed, action-oriented, transformative vision for what K–12 education must become. It's time to stop talking and start doing. Our future depends on it."

–**Rafael Pastor**, Chairman of the Board and CEO,
Vistage International, Inc.

*The New Health Age: The Future of Health Care in America*
"*The New Health Age* offers a succinct primer on how we got here and where we should be taking the health of our nation."

–**Mehmet Oz**. M.D., Host of *The Dr. Oz Show*

"*The New Health Age* provides a window for America's healthcare leaders to peer into the future and identify new ways to create high performing healthcare organizations through high impact, individualized healthcare products and services."

–**William M. Goodyear**, Chairman and Chief
Executive Officer, Navigant

# ENTERING THE SHIFT AGE

**DAVID HOULE**
AMERICA'S LEADING FUTURIST

## THE END OF THE INFORMATION AGE AND THE NEW ERA OF TRANSFORMATION

sourcebooks

Published by Sourcebooks, Inc.
P.O. Box 4410, Naperville, Illinois 60567-4410
(630) 961-3900
Fax: (630) 961-2168
www.sourcebooks.com

Library of Congress Cataloging-in-Publication Data

Houle, David.
  Entering the shift age : the end of the information age and the new era of transformation /
David Houle.
      pages cm
  Includes bibliographical references.
  1. Civilization, Modern--21st century. 2. Social history--21st century. 3. Social change. 4.
Information society. 5. Globalization--Social aspects. I. Title.
  CB430.H68 2013
  910--dc23
                                        2012040062

                     Printed and bound in the United States of America.
                          BG 10 9 8 7 6 5 4 3 2 1

To Victoria, as we fell in love all
over again during the writing of this book.

# CONTENTS

# PART 1 | WELCOME TO THE SHIFT AGE

# INTRODUCTION

Are you unsettled? Do you feel anxious about the future? Why does everything that used to work no longer work and the way that things used to be now feels long gone? Are things getting better or getting worse? Are your children coming of age at a wonderful time or a horrible time?

Well, the reason you may be feeling uneasy and asking these questions is due to the time we live in and the fact that we are at a major inflection point in human history.

We have left the Information Age and have entered a new age, the Shift Age. The Shift Age is and will be one of the most transformative times in all history. Almost everything in your life and every part of your life is in some relative rate of shift.

No wonder you are worried and anxious! Or you may be incredibly excited by the future rushing toward us. Either way, *Entering the Shift Age* is the book to better help you understand all the incredible change swirling around you. Consider this book your road map to the future.

This book also has a unique lineage.

In early 2006, I launched my futurist blog www.EvolutionShift.com with the tagline "A Future Look at Today." The reason I started the blog was simple: I had a strong sense that humanity was entering a new age—that manifestations of this new age were everywhere—and I felt the need to write about them.

The year before, when sensing that perhaps a new stage of humanity's development was underway, I went back and reread the futurists who had shaped my thinking, who, writing in the 1960s, 1970s, and 1980s, had been right about what was and would be happening in the decades ahead. These were the greats in my pantheon: Alvin Toffler and Marshall McLuhan first and foremost, along with Buckminster Fuller. Later John Naisbitt and Nicholas Negroponte wrote books built upon these greats. I even revisited the science fiction writers Arthur C. Clarke and William Gibson, as their fiction had become fact. What I found was that though these brilliant writers, particularly Toffler and McLuhan, had been incredibly insightful about the last quarter of the twentieth century, their clarity into the twenty-first century became a bit diffuse.

What was this next age? It was clear to me that the end of the Cold War, the globalization of the economy, the incredible force of the Internet, the astounding revolution in computing, and the explosive growth of cellular communications were ushering all of us into a new time that didn't yet have a name or conceptual shape.

As I researched, the word that kept coming up for me was "shift." It seemed as though a profound shift was about to occur, that there were many shifts going on that were altering humanity's reality in significant ways. How we lived, how we thought, how we perceived the world, and even our consciousness were being altered. This shift was going to be so pronounced that it seemed nothing less than an evolutionary next step. Hence the name of the blog, EvolutionShift.

As I wrote one to three columns a week, two things happened. First, my constant study, observation, and reporting from the front lines of the shift helped to shape a larger, more cohesive view of humanity's next step. Second, my blog developed a following. This ever-increasing group of followers opened doors, and brought invitations to events and conferences and then to speaking engagements. As I was developing a sense of clarity of the future, people were asking me if I was writing a book, or told me that I had to do so. So I did.

Armed with good contacts, a good agent, and a book proposal, I approached the traditional book publishing industry, though with a great sense of conflict. Here I was, a futurist, knocking at the door of an industry that clearly was about to be eviscerated due to disintermediation—and they didn't see it. The responses to my manuscript ranged from cold to ludicrous. Publishers said I was too optimistic, that the future was about apocalypse, that I needed to have the word "trend" in the title, that they already had a futurist so another one was not needed. One editor, Peter Lynch at Sourcebooks, liked my proposal but could not get unanimous agreement from the editorial committee at that time.

So, I turned to one of my favorite companies, Amazon, and had them publish *The Shift Age* in late 2007. On my blog I had forecast the coming explosive growth of ebooks, due to the probable development of a new eReader. Since this happened shortly before the Kindle was introduced, my book became available in print and ebook format by early 2008.

My life changed. Though *The Shift Age* never became a best seller in the traditional sense, it did become influential. The book made its way into the hands of CEOs, upper-level executives, and business owners. My speaking career took off—within two years of the book's first appearance on Amazon I had made some 150 speeches in several countries in North and South America. Heads of companies from around the world wrote me that the book had led them to alter the strategic vision of their enterprises. Audiences told me that my speeches changed how they looked at the world and gave them a context for understanding the scary upheaval all around them.

Simultaneously the crash of 2008 happened. Legacy thinking being what it is, most people I encountered before simply assumed we were still living in the Information Age. Now audiences were unsettled by the bursting of the housing bubble, the collapse of Lehman Brothers, and the unprecedented speed at which the world fell into the worst economic downturn in seventy years (due to the ever-increasing connectedness of the financial world). My view, that we had entered what would be a five-year reorganizational recession between two ages, was the first context that provided understanding. This great global recession was coincidental with the transition from one age, the Information Age, to the next age, the

Shift Age. In times of uncertainty, having a path to understanding at least provides perspective, if not a line of credit or a secure job.

During this time in the United States, in question-and-answer sessions after speeches, I was repeatedly asked if America would remain a great nation. I found myself answering this question by saying something along the lines of "If we don't better educate our young, if we don't become healthier, and if we don't rebuild our communications, energy, and transportation infrastructures for the twenty-first century, it doesn't matter what else we do."

Well, this led me to face America's future on those first issues and write two books. The first, *Shift Ed: A Call to Action for Transforming K–12 Education*, written with friend and coauthor Jeff Cobb and published by Corwin Press, was published in the spring of 2011 and was embraced by educators across the country. As a futurist, I challenged educators to either follow the vision set forth in the book or create their own, but that transformation was the only way forward. Many committed educators at all levels have risen to the occasion, and that transformation has begun.

The second issue-oriented book was *The New Health Age: The Future of Health Care in America*, coauthored with health care attorney Jonathan Fleece and published by Sourcebooks in January 2012. Simply put, the conversation about health care in America was and still is driven by fear, misinformation, and manipulation by politicians. The goal was to write an intelligent book to bring both intelligence and vision to the country's health care discussion. It seems to be starting to do so as of this writing.

*Entering the Shift Age* is now bringing me back to the more global, macro issues of this new Shift Age we have entered. (That third issue of infrastructure will be dealt with in the latter half of this book.) *The Shift Age* was published quickly four years ago. The goal was to get the concept of this new age out to the world in a summary form. The first quarter of that book was a general discussion of the new age, and the remaining three-quarters of the book consisted of reedited columns that I had written in my blog: the reporting from the front lines of the Shift Age. Since the publication of *The Shift Age* in early 2008, I have known that I would want to write a follow-up book that was a fuller, deeper, and more comprehensive explanation and guide to the Shift Age. This desire was driven further by the constant demand of *The Shift Age* readers for another book dealing with the larger aspects of this new age of ours.

*Entering the Shift Age* is that book.

What I had not yet figured out was how to publish this book in a way and format that was more in line with the future of publishing. This is where Dominique Raccah and Sourcebooks came in. Dominique heard me speak in mid-2011 and had a screamingly loud, full bells-and-whistles "aha moment" about publishing my work in an entirely new way. As someone who restlessly seeks new ideas and ways of doing things, Dominique had been reflecting on what new publishing models might look like. One such model was a perfect match for my book.

I came in to Sourcebooks to present to the company and to start the brainstorming of what this new publishing model would look like. Now, for the first time, I got to meet Peter Lynch, who was the only person who had wanted to say yes to my book proposal years earlier. The symmetry, serendipity, and karmic aspects of this new partnership were and are exhilarating. This book is being published using the Agile Publishing Model, which will be one of the new forms of bringing "books" to market. As a futurist, for the first time I feel the process and form match the content.

You are part of a new form of publishing. You are also now entering the Shift Age, one of the most transformative times to be alive in human history. This book, in all its electronic, print, and video aspects, will introduce the Shift Age to those of you who come to it conceptually for the first time. And for those of you who read and had your thinking changed by *The Shift Age* over these past few years, the book you hold in your hands now will give you a greater depth of understanding to these times.

We have entered the Shift Age, when almost everything is in a state of shift and change is accelerating and all around us. So, let's take a look at this new age.

David Houle
Sarasota, Florida, February 2012

# CHAPTER ONE

# WELCOME TO THE SHIFT AGE

We now live in the Shift Age, a time of transformation that will be regarded by future historians as one of the most significant periods in human history. The Shift Age is one of those inflection points or times when much of humanity will change how we live, how we think, how we interact with each other, and what we do. It will even be a time of an emerging new consciousness for many of us.

Shift is everywhere. Think about all of the shifts you're seeing happen today. How we communicate with each other. The way the new global economy is reshaping national and even local economies. What we do for a living. The values we hold. The way we raise and educate our young. The way we view the world. The way we access information and knowledge. The way we influence and are influenced by social ideas and thought.

In the Shift Age, the speed of change has accelerated to the point where change has become environmental. Change is no longer one of several dynamics that we must manage; it is the environment in which we live. We feel it. We are constantly confronted with change. The planned obsolescence of the Industrial Age has given way to the ever more rapid speed of obsolescence in technology and innovation. We now suffer from what I have called innovation fatigue.

Wait, you say, aren't we in the Information Age? Well, to some degree we still are. If the Information Age was about information, knowledge work, and computing, then yes, the Information Age is still with us. By that standard, does it mean that because we grow more food that at any time in history, we are still in the Agricultural Age? That since the global gross industrial output today is greater than ever before, we are in the Industrial Age? Actually, the answer is yes. Ages don't go away; they just become layered, sequential parts of our history of social and economic evolution. We still grow things, manufacture things, work to acquire and expand our knowledge, and live in an information-overloaded world. Yet, as we will see, the Information Age has already ceded to the Shift Age.

Humans have a unique way of looking at the present through the concepts of the past. This is legacy thinking. It is hard to avoid. We experience something, are taught something, or learn something in the past, and it then becomes the filter through which we look at and see the world. I will expand on this in Part Three of this book, as we are now going through a major collapse of legacy thinking with a speed that is unparalleled in human history. We are about to go through major shifts that will render obsolete many of the thought structures of the last 200 years. Welcome to the Shift Age.

An appropriate metaphor for the Shift Age is an earthquake. If you have ever experienced an earthquake, you know the sense of powerlessness. You can remember it as though it was yesterday. That entire drama called your life is completely forgotten. The first feeling is disorientation: what is this? Recognition that it is an earthquake instills fear, and then prompts reaction. What to do? The ground is literally shifting underfoot. You survive but are shaken. You have experienced a force greater than yourself, a turbulence you can't control. Yet you come out the other side, but with a different outlook on your life and of life in general.

Welcome to the Shift Age.

# A Very Brief History of Humanity Leading to the Shift Age

How does one age change into another? For many of us, the most immediate example we can conceive of was the change from the Industrial Age
to the Information Age. Let's take a quick contextual look back to the
beginnings of the Information Age. As the world entered the final quarter
of the twentieth century, it became clear that one age was giving way to
another. While the new age was not yet fully formed, its early manifestations suggested a clear direction. First, there was the massive increase in
college graduates in the United States, due to the GI Bill after World War
II (the Servicemen's Readjustment Act of 1944). This created a higher
percentage of the workforce with college degrees—sometimes referred to
as "knowledge workers"—than ever before. Then came the Baby Boom
generation, the transformation of the workforce from blue to white collar,
the advent of computers and their migration into everyday life, and the
launch of communications satellites, all of which presaged the onset of
something new.

The great futurist and historian Alvin Toffler called it the Third Wave,
following the previous two waves of agriculture and industry. But from
the view of the Industrial Age, it appeared that this new age was about
information, so this new time or age was christened the Information Age
by scholars, futurists, and historians alike. This name became part of the
vernacular and has been used to define our time ever since. This term, the
Information Age, is now more than thirty-five years old, and during this
time unexpected transformation has occurred.

Yet thirty-five years is actually quite a short time in the history of humanity's ages. And it is only in recent times that ages have changed so quickly.

The current iteration of humanity is known as modern humans. It is
generally accepted that the age of modern humans began some 150,000
years ago. For most of this time, humanity scarcely differed from other
animals—simply trying to survive day to day by hunting and gathering.

Then, approximately 10,000 years ago, some groups of humans
started to put down roots, and the Agricultural Age began. This led to

the place-based development of society and culture. This 10,000-year period represents most of recorded human history and is when all the great civilizations we know of came into being. The basic foundation of human society was developed during the Agricultural Age.

The Agricultural Age continued until the 1700s, when the invention of the steam engine ushered in the Industrial Age. This age brought about mechanization, urbanization, centralization, and a dramatic increase in global wealth. The Industrial Age spanned roughly 250 years until, in the last quarter of the twentieth century, the Information Age began in developed countries.

Now, let's think about the experience of change in these ages. Accept for the sake of easy math that a lifetime is 50 years. (We obviously live longer than that now, but centuries and certainly millennia ago we didn't.) If a lifetime is 50 years, then 150,000 years, the time modern humans has been on this planet, is 3,000 lifetimes. The Agricultural Age, 10,000 years in length, represents 200 lifetimes. So for the first 2,800 of modern humanity's lifetimes, we were essentially nomadic and lived in portable housing or in caves. For 200 lifetimes we tilled the land and created civilization, and for only five lifetimes we have lived in the Industrial Age with machines. Finally, it is during the life of most adults alive today that modern humans have lived in the Information Age. Modern humans therefore have spent 2,800 lifetimes living in caves, 200 lifetimes tilling the land and creating all the great civilizations of the world, five lifetimes creating all the wonders of the Industrial Age, and only a single lifetime living in the Information Age. When we look at our species in the context of this timeline, it is clear that most of what we think of when we think of "humanity" and "society" is recent.

Not only are humanity's ages fairly recent, but they are changing ever more rapidly. During the first 2,800 lifetimes, humanity had no sense of the speed of change. Survival was the only issue. Even during the Agricultural Age, the speed of change was hardly noticeable in a lifetime. People lived in the same place and held the same occupation as their parents. The average life expectancy was forty-five years or less. In the last few centuries of this age, exploration and discovery started to accelerate the social, cultural, and economic evolution around the world. The Renaissance in Europe, the great Mayan and Aztec civilizations of Central America, and the sophisticated dynasties in China and India all were toward the end of the Agricultural Age. Even during these great strides forward, humans had little or no concept of change in a lifetime.

It was not until the beginning of the Industrial Age that humanity experienced the speed of change on a large scale. In the United States, for example, if you were born in the year 1825, you grew up in an essentially agricultural society. The majority of the population lived in the country or in small towns, and land and products from it determined wealth. By your sixtieth birthday, if you lived that long, manufacturing began to supplant farming, cities were undergoing explosive growth, you could travel by train, and you could have your photograph taken. The world you lived in was noticeably different than that of your grandparents and even parents. My grandparents grew up in a world of steam engines, candlelight, and horse and buggy. I grew up in a world of television, jet planes, and communication satellites. My son grew up with video games, computers, cell phones, digital media, and the Internet.

Therefore, it is only in the last five or six lifetimes of humanity's time on earth that the speed of change could be clearly perceived to have occurred during one's life. This is essential to remember, as the awareness and experience of the speed of change as a phenomenon is common to practically every human alive today.

## The Four Ages of Humanity

While ages and stages of history often overlap and blend into each other, there are simple conceptual characteristics to every age.

> » Tools defined the Agricultural Age
> » Machines defined the Industrial Age
> » Technology defined the Information Age
> » Consciousness will define the Shift Age

That does not mean that the advancements of the previous ages go away. Clearly, in 2012 and for the foreseeable future, technology will continue to be a major influence in the world. In fact, there are tools still in use that were invented during the Agricultural Age. The same goes for Industrial Age machines. Each age adds to what has gone before, expanding and accelerating the human experience. The consciousness that will occur in the Shift Age will continue this expansion and acceleration.

New consciousness notwithstanding, it is not often clear for people living during the time that an age is changing. A new age takes root before it becomes widely understood and accepted. With the hindsight of history, we can ascertain both what events became important and when new ages gained critical mass. Even though it is generally accepted that the invention of the steam engine in the eighteenth century initiated the Industrial Age, 100 years later there were still areas of the world and entire countries that lived and operated fully in Agricultural Age economics and rhythms.

The countries that were most developed in the early part of the twentieth century were countries that had led the move from the Agricultural to the Industrial Age. In the last 100 years of the Industrial Age, the invention and rapid spreading of new forms of communications and then transport sped up the worldwide transition to this new age. The telegraph led to the telephone. Railroads increased the speed of transportation, as did the airplanes that followed. World War I was the first industrialized war, which was why it was so horrific compared to any prior war. In fact, it wasn't until during and after that war that humanity accepted it was living in this new Industrial Age.

It is also clear that the beginnings of the Information Age appeared before humanity became aware of them, and far before humanity accepted that it was living in a new age. In the 1960s, the United States was clearly an Industrial Age country. In the 1980s, it was clearly in the Information Age. The decade of the 1970s was the transition between these two ages. It was the decade of communication satellites, the personal computer, cable television, unprecedented numbers of college graduates. In other words, one could say that the Information Age began sometime around 1975. (It is generally accepted that the Industrial Age began in the 1700s and that the Information Age began sometime between 1950 and 1980. Clearly, there is no one specific date or year that an age begins, but rather a period of transition between any two historical epochs or ages. For consistency and clarity—and because I believe the demarcation between these two ages became clear in the middle of the 1970s—I arbitrarily use the date of 1975 to mark the beginning of the Information Age.) But other than futurists, visionaries, and inventors, the larger population didn't see that it was living in a new Information Age until the 1980s, when computers started to show up on desktops, the number of television channels multiplied, the majority of workers had become white collar, and the office had replaced the factory floor.

So a new age begins and develops for a time before the majority of the population perceives that it is living in it. I submit that the Shift Age began around 2006 or the middle of the last decade. It has been interesting to me that, when I first started to speak about this new age in 2007, people had a hard time perceiving that they were in a new age. By 2011, during a four-year reorganizational recession, audiences have largely accepted that a new age might well be upon us, as everything had changed or shifted so much in such a short period of time.

This does not mean that when people realize a new age has begun they easily accept it. When a new age is born, it seems radical and transformative, and it is often resisted as unnatural, non-human, immoral, or threatening. This is due to the very nature of human thought. We know what we know; we live in a time when things are the way they are. To think differently is difficult. Truth as we have known it is shown to not be true. We find out that facts that we've accepted are not really facts, but beliefs.

Ten thousand years ago, the radical idea slowly emerged of humans staying in one place, growing food, and creating the tools to do so. Staying in one place and not following the animals and the weather must have seemed almost unnatural. The introduction of the Agricultural Age took many millennia to become dominant. Once it was, then towns and cities superseded migrant tribes. These led to the development of the Concept of Place. People spent entire lives living in a single place for the first time in humankind's time on Earth.

Once lives started to revolve around place, then civilization began. Social rules, culture, and mores were established to organize these place-based, agriculturally driven civilizations. Place became defining. People were from a place. This led to the orientation of land as the dominant form of wealth. Wealth came from the land.

The Industrial Age triggered massive change. People left the land for the rapidly growing cities. Machines became dominant. Factories created a centralized workforce. The concepts of jobs and management began. The factory was the model, and production superseded the land as a form and measurement of wealth creation. Those who controlled production created unprecedented wealth. Robber Barons in most countries amassed vast wealth and created hundreds of thousands of (often low-paying) jobs. Land was no longer solely the place on which crops were grown but the place from which minerals and fossil fuels were extracted. Cities grew explosively as the poor who worked the land before could now earn more money in cities and factories.

The Industrial Age gave us all the machines and inventions we now take for granted: automobiles, electricity, elevators, airplanes, and untold numbers of production-related types of machinery. This economic reorganization initiated new social organizations, such as public school systems, transportation systems, private clubs, civic and charity organizations, organized sports, and of course everything related to the automobile. Simply put, the Industrial Age organized the developed countries of the world into an order that, in large part, defined the nineteenth and twentieth centuries (and is still largely in place today).

The Industrial Age moved the concept of Place from small towns and the land to the city. Along with this move, of course, was the introduction of communication inventions that became systems that made the world "smaller." The telegraph was replaced by the telephone. Radio was followed by television. The world became more connected. World War II was the first radio war. Vietnam was the first television war.

Then, in the 1970s, high technology started to replace machines. Computers moved from big air-conditioned basements to the desktop. Communication satellites increased global communication and created such businesses as cable television. Computers dramatically increased everything in science, business, and education. The fax machine, the electronic calculator, and the copier changed the office. The appearance of these devices in our daily life and work was when we realized that this newly named Information Age was upon us.

Since the Information Age began approximately forty years ago in developed countries, the perception of change and the speed of change have become pronounced. The future has seemed to show up at an accelerating rate. Alvin Toffler's book *Future Shock* was published in 1970. The simple premise of the book was that humanity was entering a period when time is accelerating, and new inventions will show up and "shock" us into the future. One personal example was when, in the mid-1980s, I saw a man walking down the street talking on one of those early five-pound cell phones. Wow, a phone without a cord being used on the street! That is the future!

In the decades since 1970, humanity has come to accept this future shock as an almost constant experience. We settle into learning and adapting to a new technology and its enabling power in our lives, and then almost immediately a new technological breakthrough or gadget renders what we just mastered dated or even obsolete. We say we embrace innovation, and yet at times it overwhelms us. We want to keep up, and in most areas of our lives we do, but there always seems to be a part of our lives where we can't quite catch up. Things move at us too fast and with great force, as though we are drinking from the proverbial fire hose. This sense of the rapidity of change really began in the past twenty-five years, a transitional time when humanity moved from what was to what will be.

Change can be quite unsettling. What we "know" and the technologies we use are our current reality. We all tend to develop a sense of comfort in what is, what is known, how we live, and what the current parameters and ways of living are. So when we feel some change or sense of disruption, we often get anxious. In reality, the only constant in the universe is change. In modern humans' most recent history, the speed of change and the depth of the sense of disruption have been increasing.

So, let us take a look at the twenty-year period that will be looked upon as the demarcation line between the past and the present/future.

# CHAPTER TWO

# THE THRESHOLD DECADES

**threshold**

1: the plank, stone, or piece of timber that lies under a door: sill

2 a: gate, door b (1): end, boundary; specifically: the end of a runway (2): the place or point of entering or beginning: outset "on the threshold of a new age"

3 a: the point at which a physiological or psychological effect begins to be produced "has a high threshold for pain" b: a level, point, or value above which something is true or will take place and below which it is not or will not

—Merriam-Webster Online Dictionary

A threshold is a place of entering or beginning. It is a place between two rooms, a doorway. *Threshold* is also used in the context of pain, as in one's "pain threshold." All three meanings pertain to the Threshold Decades, the twenty-year period from 1985 to 2005.

The years from 1985 to 2005 were a time of incredible change. In fact, it is hard to find another twenty-year period in the history of humanity when our world changed as much in such a short period of time. Fifty years from now, I believe these two decades will be seen as a true demarcation in the history of humanity, an obvious time bridge between two eras.

Practically every aspect of life changed. Since there has been so much transformation, change, and innovation, it is easy to forget what actually happened during these twenty years. Here is a quick look at 1985:

» The political and economic world was divided in two: the Eastern Bloc, controlled by the Soviet Union, and the Western Bloc, led by the United States.

» China was the world's largest communist nation, with closed and protected borders.

» The precursor to the Internet was used by only a few thousand people, mostly in scientific, academic, and governmental settings.

» The first cell phones were appearing, but they weighed several pounds, and there were just a few hundred thousand users.

» The personal computer was in the very early stages of distribution and existed mostly in business settings.

» The fax machine was just gaining distribution.

» There were three broadcast networks in the United States.

» The penetration of cable television into households in the United States was under 40 percent, and there were fewer than twenty cable networks.

Those of you who went through this twenty-year period as adults look back on this and are amazed how much has changed. You have adapted and accepted so much newness into your lives that the snapshot of reality above makes you realize how much change we have experienced. Those of you who were young children or were born during the Threshold Decades now can see how different your lives as adults are today from those of your parents.

# Major Transformations in the Threshold Decades

Much has been written about the movement from analog to digital, from hierarchies to networks, from few to many, from fast to faster, and from national to global. I do not intend to rehash or deeply investigate these subjects. This book, after all, is about macro trends, the largest forces reorganizing our world. That said, a brief recap is constructive, not only to provide a refresher on all that happened during this twenty-year period, but also to set the stage for the Shift Age, which follows the Threshold Decades.

## ANALOG TO DIGITAL

Between 1985 and 2005, developed countries moved from analog to digital. This shift underpins the technological communications growth and computing explosion cited earlier. It is also evident in music's moving from analog LPs and tapes to CDs to digital downloading. The same parallel occurred in film with the move from VHS to DVD to digital downloading. Digital downloading greatly increased Internet use, caused upheaval in the affected industries, and disintermediated professions.

The conversion to digital also accelerated access and usage. A consumer can go right to her favorite song on the CD or scene on the DVD, without waiting for fast-forwarding. This has created an expectation among consumers of immediacy and "on demand" fulfillment, which

## 1985

If you were a middle-aged American in 1985, you most likely:

» Had a repressed fear of a nuclear war with the Soviet Union that would destroy both nations and most of the world.
» Had a phone at home and one at the office, both attached to the wall.
» Had in your entire office complex one or two personal computers that somebody had been specially trained to operate.
» Had maybe a single, slow fax machine in your workplace.
» Were in the 40 percent of the population that had a VCR, and most of what you viewed you recorded (with difficulty) as there were few video rental stores.
» Listened to music on vinyl records or cassettes.
» Rarely experienced what is now called "airport security."
» Most likely had never heard of AIDS or HIV, and had certainly never heard of Al Qaeda, outsourcing, downsizing, cheap airfares, DNA mapping, or the Internet.

now drives consumer and individual empowerment. Music can instantly be downloaded to wherever you are. Movies are increasingly streamed, videos instantly served up for viewing. All forms of content are available right here, right now. We determine what and when, and often how much—always on, always available.

## HIERARCHIES TO NETWORKS

In 1985 the world was still largely structured around hierarchies. The drive toward centralization that occurred during the Industrial Age created hierarchies in business, government, and practically any large organization. In fact, half of the world, the Eastern Bloc, operated with central planning committees. Even in the social realm, there were pecking orders, remnants of the aristocracies of the Agricultural Age, and economic social structures held over from the robber barons of the Industrial Age.

These hierarchies were challenged and, in many cases, converted or obliterated during the Threshold Decades, when most of society started to reorganize around the network structure. Vertical hierarchies flattened into horizontal networks. Decision-making was pushed down in organizations, rendering hierarchy less important. The new connectedness allowed people to circumvent traditional social structures and connect around common interests, regardless of location. In 1985, people worked up the corporate ladder and socialized at private clubs. In 2005, people worked as independent contractors or entrepreneurs, connecting on online social networks.

Our world is now one of networks. Hierarchies still exist, particularly in government, but they are no longer as respected and are often scorned for being slow-moving. In fact, all the areas of society that still had a great amount of bureaucracy in 2005 and have not yet radically changed are suffering ever lowering respect and slowing ability to keep up.

## FEW TO MANY: THE TRIUMPH OF CHOICE

Along with the transition from hierarchies to networks came the shift from few to many. Even on the political front, numbers increased. In

1985, there were 159 member nations of the United Nations. In 2005, there were 191, largely due to the fragmenting of the Soviet Union into fifteen countries and Yugoslavia into five. In existing democracies, new political parties were created, often issue-oriented ones such as the various environmentally focused Green parties that have sprung up in several developed countries. Democratic choices increased.

Media is perhaps the clearest example of the explosion of choice. In 1985, the United States had three broadcast networks and approximately twenty cable networks. In 2005, there were six broadcast networks and more than 100 cable networks. The number of websites went from a handful to millions.

| Number (in the U.S.) | 1950 | 1975 | 1985 | 1995 | 2005 |
|---|---|---|---|---|---|
| Radio Stations | 2,232 | 4,463 | 8,593 | 11,987 | 13,499 |
| Websites | | | 0 | 23,500 | 75,251,156 |
| Published Books | 11,022 | 39,372 | 75,452 | 113,589 | 251,903 |
| TV Channels (Average Household) | 2 | 3 | 18 | 41 | 102 |

Figure 1: The Explosion of Choice in the United States: 1950–2005[1]

While this movement from few to many occurred, new technologies came to market that helped the consumer make selections. During the growth of television viewing options, the remote control came to market: the viewer could change channels without getting up from the couch. The remote control helped the consumer make fast and immediate decisions. This loss of command was the beginning of the end of network programmers' command over viewers. This loss of command also happened with digital purchase of music, allowing the buyer to select single tracks and therefore unbundle the album concept.

The key development that came from the transition of few to many was the explosion of choice for everyone. With hundreds of channels, tens of thousands of books, millions of websites, and even dozens of different toothpastes, the consumer had an ever-increasing amount of choice and therefore control. Today, more than any time in history, the consumer has the power of choice and uses that power every day.

Today, in the Shift Age, the power of the individual is growing every day. As we will see in Chapter Four of this book, we as individuals have more power today than individuals have ever had. It was during the Threshold Decades that the explosion of choice began. This means that the power has moved from the producer to the consumer, from the institution to the individual.

## EVER FASTER

During the Threshold Decades, everything seemed to move faster and faster. Cell phones, the Internet, and personal computers drove this acceleration. The speed of computers doubled every eighteen to twenty-four months. The back-and-forth nature of most human communication collapsed. The turnaround time for mailing a letter and receiving a response was approximately a week; the turnaround time for sending and receiving an email was minutes, and instant messaging only took seconds. Waiting for someone to get home or get to the office to return a phone call was no longer necessary; you called the person wherever she was. This time shortening increased the velocity of transactions, business decisions, and plans (teenagers now make plans moment to moment via text messaging). Decisions happened much faster in a networked, decentralized environment than in a hierarchical, centralized one. Work could be done much more quickly on faster computers.

When Internet usage took off during the second half of the Threshold Decades, people could work around the clock. Suffer from insomnia in the middle of the night? Send emails. Financial projections need to be reworked? Have them back on the boss's electronic desk before she logs on in the morning. Work became something one could do 24/7.

Communications became closer to immediate than ever before. All this connectedness accelerated human interaction. Factor in the constant and rapid rate of innovation across numerous fields: medicine, science, non-human space exploration, artistic creation, most forms of content publishing, and any number of other fields underwent significant advancement, accelerating the general speed of change to a rate never before experienced.

By the end of the Threshold Decades, the speed of change had accelerated so much that it was no longer sequential (as in the Industrial Age) but had become simultaneous across multiple social areas. This set the stage for the Shift Age, where change becomes part of our environment. We now live in an environment of change.

## WEST MEETS EAST

The social, economic, and political ramifications of the unification of the Eastern Bloc and the Western Bloc cannot be overstated. In 1985, communism was perceived as a possible economic and political order. By 2005, it was essentially dead as a viable way of governance. The largest communist country in the world in terms of population, China, became the fastest growing capitalistic economy in the world. In 1985, there was no real global economy. In 2005, there was a vibrant global economy. In 1985, there was minimal and highly controlled economic activity between the Eastern and Western Blocs. In 2005, Europe used millions of barrels of Russian oil, and the United States was awash in products made in China. The collapse of communism, most symbolically represented by the tearing down of the Berlin Wall, created a vacuum, and global forces rushed in. For the first time since before World War I, the economic movement toward a global economy resumed and then took off.

So it was during this post–Cold War time that the West began to aggressively export its capitalistic way of life. Western companies set up international supply chains utilizing newly opened countries and markets for low-cost production. Western consumer culture was widely embraced by former Eastern communist countries. This started the creation of rapidly growing numbers of people in the middle class around the world.

There was another merger of East and West that was equally profound, although perhaps less noticeable. This was the merger of underlying beliefs and philosophies. During the second half of the twentieth century, culminating in the Threshold Decades, Western science, particularly in the fields of particle and quantum physics, reached several core conclusions. Drilling down into ever-smaller subatomic particles, physicists realized that everything, at its core, is energy. For centuries, Eastern philosophy, medicine and religion had been based on the belief that everything was energy. Finally, as predicted by several thinkers who had bridged Eastern and Western thinking, the two schools of thought ended up at the same place: All Is One.

Thus, not only had the economic, political, and social barriers to the movement to global order come to an end during the Threshold Decades, a partial unification of the underlying tenets of Western scientific thought and Eastern philosophical thought had come together. The obvious cultural manifestation of this in the United States and Europe was the explosive growth of such practices as yoga and meditation and the Dalai Lama's and Deepak Chopra's scaling the best-seller lists. Humanity was on the path to becoming one.

In the Threshold Decades, while the West was busy exporting its capitalistic and economic way of life to the East, the East was exporting its more integrated, holistic, and contextual way of thinking. So globalism was more than just an economic reorganization and integration, it was the emerging new reality of thought and behavior.

We now look at what was unquestionably the single greatest development of the Threshold Decades, the one that has created an entirely new environment and changed humanity forever. Literally, the accepted time, space, and place underpinnings of humanity were being altered. These new technologies—which are now as of this writing commonly accepted—were disruptive and almost unfathomable when first introduced. In addition, the rapidity of growth of these new technologies was historically unprecedented.

## EXPLOSIVE GROWTH IN TECHNOLOGICAL CONNECTEDNESS

The Threshold Decades were not only a period of fundamental change, but also a time when technologies developed and brought to market in the previous decades experienced explosive growth.

| Number (Worldwide) | 1950 | 1975 | 1985 | 1995 | 2005 |
|---|---|---|---|---|---|
| Computers | 60 | 500,000 | 30,373,576 | 207,365,651 | 1,425,000,000 |
| Cell Phone Subscribers | | | 750,629 | 89,978,977 | 2,109,960,723 |
| Internet Users | | | 210,000 | 45,100,000 | 1,094,000,000 |

FIGURE 2. GLOBAL TECHNOLOGY GROWTH: 1950 TO 2005[2]

| Number (in the U.S.) | 1950 | 1975 | 1985 | 1995 | 2005 |
|---|---|---|---|---|---|
| Computers | 9 | 400,000 | 25,270,000 | 86,300,000 | 203,700,000 |
| Cell Phone Subscribers | | | 340,213 | 33,785,660 | 201,650,000 |
| Internet Users | | | 190,000 | 28,100,000 | 205,327,000 |

FIGURE 3. TECHNOLOGY GROWTH IN THE UNITED STATES: 1950 TO 2005[3]

The exponential growth in number of computers between 1975 and 1985 was largely due to the introduction of the first personal computers. Before this time, most computers were mainframes or minicomputers used exclusively by institutions. As these numbers indicate, the Threshold Decades were clearly a time when computers went from being something special for business to being commonplace and for everyone.

The truly remarkable numbers in Figures 2 and 3 are those regarding cell phones and Internet use. Both technologies went from early stages to full market penetration and acceptance, providing electronic connectedness to the world.

At the beginning of the Threshold Decades, in 1985, humanity was not connected except via landline phones, and it was only in developed countries that these landlines were used by a majority of households. In 2005, more than 2 billion people had cell phones; not only were there more phones in use around the world, but they were portable. Communication ceased to be tied to place as it had been in 1985.

This was an extremely important transition, as it made human communication completely mobile for the first time in history. People could be anywhere and be connected. And this is now occurring globally. While the United States represented close to 50 percent of all cell phones in 1985, that percentage was down to 10 percent in 2005. The cell phone had become a global technology.

The growth in Internet usage was even greater. In 1985, the Internet was not available to the public; so all traffic was institutional. By 2005, the increasing connectedness of the world collapsed time and distance in the realm of human communication. This connectedness was simultaneous and parallel to the massive social, political, and economic forces that were unleashing globalism around the world. It is interesting to note that, as with cell phones, the United States was dominant in Internet usage in 1985, with 90 percent of all users, but by 2005 that percentage had dropped to 20 percent. The world was quickly adapting to this new 24/7 electronic medium. The transformation was creating a "global village" vaster and more interactive than anything Marshall McLuhan, the man who coined the phrase in the 1960s, could have foreseen.

The global village of electronic communications created during the Threshold Decades was not due just to the exponential growth in the number of users of cell phones, the Internet, and computers. The constant innovation in all these technologies was an ongoing phenomenon. Moore's Law—the theory developed by Gordon Moore, founder of Intel, in 1965, that states that computing power and speed double every eighteen months while at the same time drops in price by half—became a living reality. Every year or two there was a new generation of computers that were smaller, faster, more powerful, and cheaper. This not only fed the rapid growth of the PC market, it also dramatically increased speed and productivity in business. As computer capability dramatically increased, it affected the explosive growth of Internet usage as the download speeds for modem dial-up increased every year. Paralleling this was the miniaturization of cell phones that were increasingly feature-rich. By 2005, PCs, cell phones, cell phone contracts, and access to the Internet had dropped in price so much compared to even a few years earlier that all these technologies became commodities. The cell phone went from being a cutting-edge, transformative, expensive piece of technology to being a disposable consumer product. All of this greatly affected usage patterns.

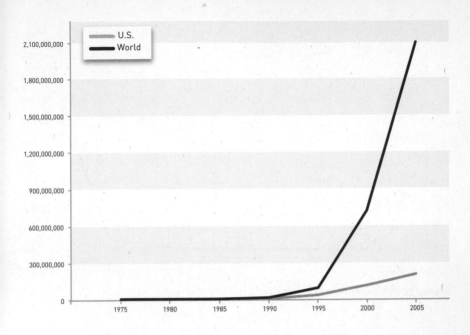

FIGURE 4. CELL PHONE SUBSCRIBERS IN U.S. AND WORLD[2]

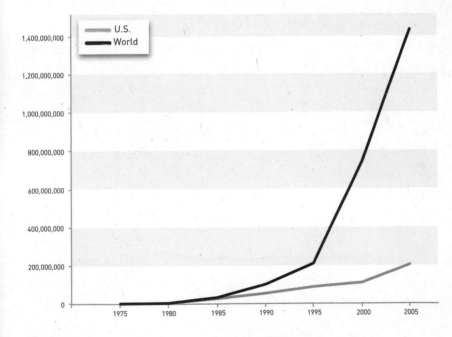

FIGURE 5. NUMBER OF COMPUTERS IN U.S. AND WORLD[2]

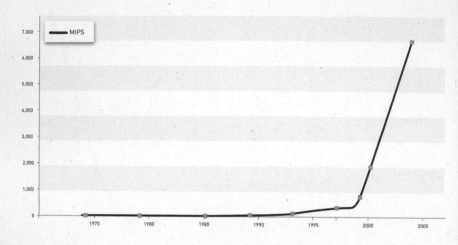

FIGURE 6. MICROPROCESSOR POWER IN MIPS, 1975–2005[4]

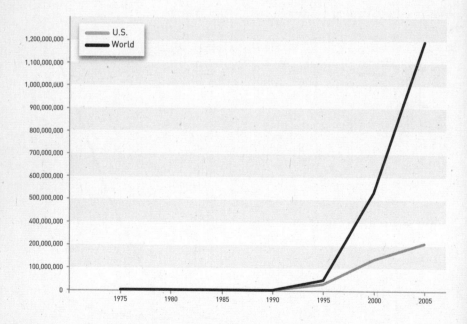

FIGURE 7. NUMBER OF INTERNET USERS IN THE U.S. AND WORLD[2]

FIGURE 8. U.S. AND WORLD INTERNET TRAFFIC, IN TERABYTES, 1985–2005[5]

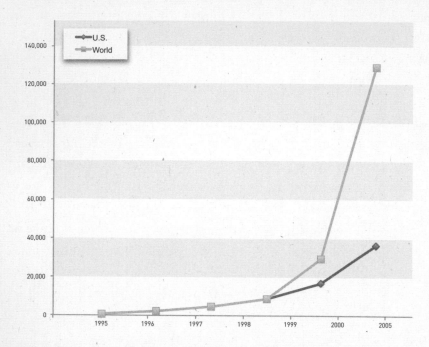

FIGURE 9. U.S. AND WORLD INTERNET TRAFFIC, IN TERABYTES, 1995–2005

There are several key points conveyed in these graphs. All three technologies—cell phones, Internet, and PCs—displayed accelerating growth curves during the Threshold Decades. The rate of growth was greatest during the last five years of the Threshold Decades. The growth of cell phones, computers, and Internet usage occurred simultaneously. The growth of these technologies was global, and while the United States initially had an advantage, the rest of the world started to both catch up and then exceed the United States in rates of growth.

Not only did connectedness dramatically increase as more people joined, the speed and amount of information being communicated also dramatically increased. So, more people became connected, and as they did so, they also created more information and content.

There has never been another twenty-year period in human history when this amount of transformation in the way human beings communicate with each other occurred. In this regard, the Threshold Decades represent a singular time in history. A level of human connectedness existed at the end of this twenty-year period that not only was new but was practically unthinkable decades ago, except perhaps in the pages of science fiction.

## Summary of the Threshold Decades

The twenty-year period of 1985–2005 was a time of significant transition from the accepted "reality" of the past to the new "reality" of the present. It was a time when the triumphs and constructs of the twentieth century came up against the new global realities of the twenty-first century.

During this two-decade time, widely accepted ways of doing business, well-entrenched distribution systems and models, and economic constructs, were challenged, altered, and in some cases eviscerated. Many industries that were perceived as dynamic, powerful, and well situated in 1985 were on life support by 2005. Entire businesses were rendered obsolete in record time.

The Threshold Decades will truly be seen by future historians as the demarcation between the room of the past and the room of the present. Between the room of what was and the room of what is and what will be.

This twenty-year period was the transition not only to this new century and to this new millennium, but also to this new age we now find ourselves in: the Shift Age.

# PART 2 | THE THREE FORCES OF THE SHIFT AGE

# INTRODUCTION

Every new age is ushered in by a confluence of forces that disrupt and alter society.

The primary force of the Agricultural Age—agriculture—changed how humans lived in terms of diet and created the Concept of Place and the beginnings of society and civilization. The initial forces of mechanization and centralization of the Industrial Age drove urbanization and the creation of rapidly growing cities around the world. These also created hierarchical management structures in business that had only existed in the military. This change led not only to the establishment of management theory, but the concept of the "job." The forces of subsidized higher education on a massive scale, satellites, and the development of computers and the rapid spread of them throughout the world initiated the Information Age.

It is no different with the Shift Age—you can feel the force of change in every part of our life and world today. In fact, the Shift Age is being created and shaped by three major forces:

» The Flow to Global
» The Flow to the Individual
» Accelerating Electronic Connectedness

Now, that isn't to say there aren't many other dynamics and influences defining our world today: religious fundamentalism, climate change, energy, poverty, migration, and overpopulation, to name just a few. But the preceding three forces are the dominant ones that are reshaping humanity in the Shift Age. Most of the disruptive changes and disorienting speed of change we all experience can, to a great degree, be traced back to these three forces.

It is hard to think of a business or human endeavor that has not been and is not being affected by these forces. Whether in the real estate industry, the communications industry, print and electronic media companies, retailing, energy, cultural institutions, or the medical and education sectors, everyone sees the clear effects and dramatic changes coming from these three forces.

And these forces are affecting our personal lives too. Think about how the global economy and globalism have impacted what you do. Think about how much power you have today as an individual and how you use it. Think about how differently you communicate and how connected you are to people all around the world.

Next we will take a close look at each of these three forces—the Flow to Global, the Flow to the Individual, and Accelerating Electronic Connectedness—to see how they are shaping our lives and our business, and how we can grasp their power as we enter the Shift Age.

# CHAPTER THREE

# THE FLOW TO GLOBAL

As was the case for all three forces, the seeds of the Flow to Global were launched in the Threshold Decades. The end of the Cold War and the collapse of the Eastern Bloc created an opening for globalism to take root, launching a rapid growth of the global economy. The coming together of Eastern and Western thought created a more unified and integrated way for humanity to think and live. The move from hierarchies to networks flattened corporations and allowed them to move outward horizontally. Global supply chains were developed. All of this new globalism swelled into the force known as the Flow to Global.

Today in the Shift Age, humanity is heading toward a new global integration. In our history, we moved through geographical stages in how we identified our place in regards to others: first family, then tribe, village, city, state, and country. Now, due to our sheer numbers and our increasing electronic connectedness, we have arrived at a point when we will all consider ourselves part of one global community.

This is a new phenomenon. Even in the later part of the twentieth century, we often used the word "international" rather than "global." We traveled internationally or had international business relationships. But today, the words "foreign" and "international" have given way to the word "global," and we find ourselves integrating this new emerging sense of global citizenship with our past identities.

How did this happen? First, there are simply so many more of us today. The population explosion means we no longer feel as though we live far apart from other groups of people, but together in a dense population. Next, economics historically leads the way in the change of an era, followed by politics and culture. And today we are ever more rapidly becoming a global economy. Finally, along with the economic changes, historically unprecedented growth in electronic connectivity helped to accelerate this new Flow to Global in politics and culture. When the speed of communications accelerated, the world became smaller. Borders opened; boundaries collapsed, and culture and world politics rushed in. Hundreds of millions of people and then billions of people for the first time were exposed to information and opportunity that were global in scope. There was a massive increase in migration, as workers from poorer countries went to richer countries to work for significantly higher wages that could be sent home or used to move the entire family to a new land of opportunity. Distinct national identities started to blur as most nations experienced ever more multicultural integration.

Let's take a close look at each of these factors, to better understand how we became global citizens and what it means for our future.

## Population

It took modern humans approximately 150,000 years to reach a global population of 1 billion. This roughly coincided with the end of the Agricultural Age. But during the Industrial Age, another 3 billion people were added, so that by the beginning of the Information Age in 1975, there were 4 billion of us. There were roughly 5 billion at the start of the Threshold Decades and approximately 6½ billion at the dawn of the Shift Age.

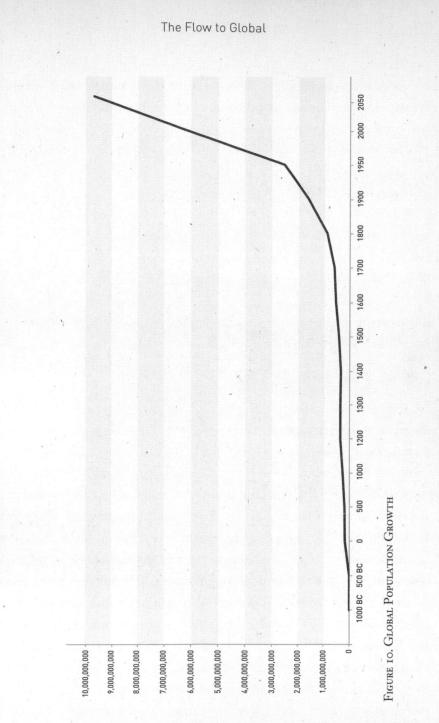

FIGURE 10. GLOBAL POPULATION GROWTH

What we see in Figure 11 (on the next page) is the exact year human-ity reached each billion milestone and the number of years between each milestone. What becomes obvious is the ever more rapid rate at which milestone is reached. Only now in 2012, when this book is being written, are we beginning to see a lengthening of time between billions.

| Year | World Population | Years in Between |
|------|-----------------|------------------|
| 1804 | 1,000,000,000 | |
| 1927 | 2,000,000,000 | 123 |
| 1960 | 3,000,000,000 | 33 |
| 1974 | 4,000,000,000 | 14 |
| 1987 | 5,000,000,000 | 13 |
| 1999 | 6,000,000,000 | 12 |
| 2011 | 7,000,000,000 | 14 |
| 2025 | 8,000,000,000 | 15 |
| 2045 | 9,000,000,000 | 26 |
| 2083 | 10,000,000,000 | 38 |

FIGURE 11. MILESTONES IN WORLD POPULATION: WHEN DID/WILL WE REACH THE NEXT BILLION?

No wonder we have entered the global stage of human evolution—there are simply so many of us! Two hundred years ago, when the Industrial Age was impacting the world, there were only a few cities with a million or more inhabitants. Most of the rest of the world consisted of small towns and wide-open spaces. We felt there was open space if we wanted it. As we entered the Information Age, the combination of explosive population growth and early understandings of the finiteness of the planet made us sense that impending limits lay ahead. As we now enter the Shift Age, the 7 billion of us are experiencing the consequences of our physical presence—gridlock, congestion, pollution—and our ever-accelerating virtual connectedness to each other.

The growth in our population though, while still rapid, is beginning to change. As nations develop and become more urban, birthrates are going down. The population replacement rate is 2.1 children per childbearing woman. This number was reached in most developed countries of the world by the latter part of the twentieth century. The less developed countries had much higher birthrates for many reasons. Now that the global economy is moving many countries from the category of less developed and rural to developed and urban, the global birthrate is declining. As Figure 12 shows, the population explosion that began in the middle of the twentieth century will level off by the middle of the twenty-first century. Still, in this 100-year period, our species will have more than tripled in number—imagine the density and connectedness we'll all feel in the next three decades!

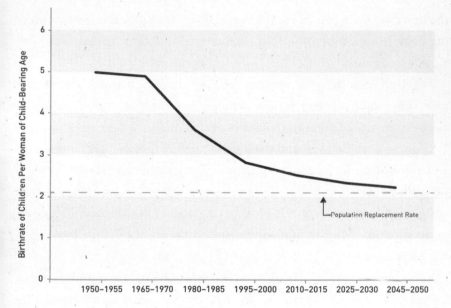

FIGURE 12. DECLINING FERTILITY RATES

So, the Flow to Global is propelled in part by the simple fact that there are so many of us living on planet Earth at the highest gross global population density in history.

# Economics First

In any major change in human history, you will almost always see an economic factor leading the way before the change reaches politics and culture. For example, the ancient conquerors expanded empires to gain control of more land, more people, and the riches that could be created from the land. Economics was often the initial driver.

The Flow to Global we are experiencing today was first manifested with the beginnings and rapid growth of the now global economy. When the Eastern Bloc collapsed, first with the symbolic destruction of the Berlin Wall in 1989 and later with the disintegration of the Soviet Union in the early 1990s, the new global economy began to really take off. For the first time since before World War I, there was a global economic playing field. In fact, most of us first encountered the term "globalization" in a business context.

This global economic playing field presents both opportunity and pain. The pain has been felt quite strongly in recent years, from recession to the disintermediation of industries. When industries go away, there is the pain of both that loss and the loss of comfort that the way things used to be no longer is. In countries such as the United States, what used to be great no longer is, and there is a reactive urge to go back to recapture old glories. This, of course, is a losing proposition. As Marshall McLuhan famously said, "Most of humanity drive on the freeway of life looking in the rearview mirror."

The opportunities, though, are both readily apparent and in rapid creation. Where old models of an industry go away, the compensating growth of the new business formations create optimism and a new sense of empowerment. We are all given a new opportunity to grow economically in ways we couldn't imagine just a few years ago.

The economic status of the world is changing as well. The world is rapidly moving from the Industrial and even Information Age model of "have" and "have not" nations to a new reality of all countries moving to "haves." The language has even changed—we now are replacing the term "third world" with "developing." In the newly developed and developing countries there is an incredible upswing in affluence and increased standard of living. Globally, tens of millions of people are entering the middle class for the first time every year. This huge expansion of the middle class creates market demand, which of course fuels the increasing rate of global economic activities in new transborder ways.

We are economically becoming organized around all of us, the "macro-macro." Today there is no bigger economic entity than all of us.

# Culture and Politics

Just as changes in politics and culture almost always follow in the wake of economic change, we will see a new global culture and politics follow global economics. Both in fact are already becoming globalized, and will continue to do so at an ever-increasing rate. This will complete the Flow to Global: a complete reorganization of humanity around the global concept.

The roots of our move from national to global orientation in our culture and politics can be found in the exploration and resultant colonialism of recent centuries. In fact, you can still see the remnants of these past empires today: the countries of the British Commonwealth in many cases drive on the left side of the road, and Brazil speaks Portuguese as a legacy of the Portuguese Empire, while the rest of South America speaks Spanish as a legacy of the Spanish Empire.

The twentieth-century inventions of radio and then television, more than any prior technologies or inventions, connected national populations and helped make the world smaller. Hearing Edward R. Murrow's voice live from London during the Battle of Britain brought World War II into the living rooms of America. The launches of manned space missions at Cape Canaveral were televised live around the world. The concept of time in relation to distance was profoundly altered. The electric global village envisioned by Marshall McLuhan became the new environment in which humanity began to live.

The sharing of culture rapidly increased as we moved from the 1960s to the twenty-first century. The Beatles, the youth counterculture movement in America, and animation from Japan are all examples of culture that developed massive followings around the world. Today, unique national cultures are increasingly being usurped by the global culture. The indigenous and folk cultures that used to define a country are becoming legacy cultures preserved through rituals and holidays, while the global culture becomes ever more pervasive and prevalent on a day-to-day basis.

The changes in politics and government are a bit harder to see, as government is now the slowest moving part of society. Today, the government of almost any country moves more slowly than do the entrepreneurs, corporations, and general public. It is the most bureaucratic and institutionalized part of society, influenced by existing special interests and largely filled with long-term workers. There is not a developed country of the world whose government is not largely of the Industrial Age in construct and function.

Accelerating connectivity will eventually force governments to pick up the pace, because government is increasingly on display and can be petitioned more quickly. Still, it often feels as though government leaders have become followers. The phrase "national leaders" is becoming oxymoronic in this new global age.

The Flow to Global is creating a world where the nation-state, that great invention of the Industrial Age, is becoming an anachronism. A powerful nation-state with centralized power was necessary to aggregate smaller units of people into countries that provided identity, services, safety, education, and economic force. In the global age, nation-states are out of step, stuck in times past.

What will the next stage of government be? The United Nations has performed its duty as well as possible throughout the Cold War and into the new millennium. It, however, is an organization composed of nation-states, nation-states with their own agendas, political and economic. Issues and crises tend to get addressed from the self-serving viewpoints of the nation-states.

Increasingly the major issues facing the citizens of the world are global in scope. Global issues need global answers. Global warming and climate change is a primary example. There is absolutely no way any nation-state can solve this problem alone. The entire world needs to be involved in solving this problem.

Eventually, issues such as global warming, ocean restoration, allocation of natural resources such as water, space exploration, the energy crisis, the extinction of plant and animal species, and overall geographic and environmental degradation will result in the creation of global agencies, empowered to coordinate efforts to address and solve these problems. And this will accelerate the movement toward the development of a global government.

Sometime in the next ten years, there will be the creation of a new global governing body that will be both an outgrowth of these global issue–oriented organizations and a successor to the increasingly irrelevant and gridlocked United Nations. This entity, which I will call the Global Council, could be charged with oversight of planetary issues, leaving the United Nations to manage and adjudicate political and economic disputes between nations. National governments will be left with the responsibilities for services, infrastructure, the safety of their citizens, and the maintenance of historical national heritage.

This Global Council will be created during the Shift Age. As all past economic and social entities such as towns, cities, countries, states, and nations created governmental structures in their own time, so the Flow to Global will necessitate the creation of this Global Council.

This will be hard for many to see or accept, as all reading these words have some sense, mild to strong, of nationality. One's sense of one's nationality may well continue, but it will be less restrictive and oppositional, and more something that defines where one is from and has grown up. Prior to the Industrial Age, Europe was a collection of aristocratic fiefdoms where marriage served as the bonds of unity. When this new age birthed large cities, the view of one's identity moved from monarchy to democracy and from region to nation, introducing the 300-year apotheosis of the nation-state. This will now move to a larger, more integrated global construct as the politics of the world are pulled by the global economy into this new age.

We already have a global culture in rapid development. Prior to the Shift Age, media were national, communications were national, and distance and place to some degree corralled culture within national boundaries. Now, the Internet provides global cultural connectivity, so that cultures and people become ever more connected and integrated. The silos of national distribution that existed are largely gone, and all forms of culture now flow around the world at the speed of light. The direction is clear that increasingly we are developing global cultural integration.

## The Global Stage of Human Evolution

With the global economic changes underway and the resultant social changes taking root, we are developing the identity of global citizens. Whether one has come to this new identity through one's business or line of work or through political or cultural issues, we all, to varying degrees, see ourselves as global citizens. Globalization is no longer simply an economic term; it is the term of what is and what will course through all aspects of human society for the ten to twenty years of the Shift Age.

The population growth of the last fifty years, the rapidly integrated global economy, the issue-led globalization of politics, and the flow of culture around the world via the Internet point us to the next step.

We have entered the global stage of human evolution.

# CHAPTER FOUR

# THE FLOW TO THE INDIVIDUAL

The changes that occurred during the Threshold Decades also triggered a transfer of power in our society from large groups to each person—what I refer to as the Flow to the Individual.

Power has migrated from institutions to individuals due to the explosion of choice, the growth of free agency, the technologies and dynamics moving us from hierarchies to networks, and ever-increasing electronic connectedness. Gatekeepers are disappearing; disintermediation—and its primary agent, the Internet—are reorganizing the economic landscape. The individual is becoming the primary economic unit, the micro-micro that is combining with the macro-macro of the Flow to Global. We are distinct individuals who are also global citizens.

## Free Agents

The Flow to the Individual can, in part, be traced to the movement from a production economy that was hierarchical to a knowledge- and information-based economy that is flat and networked. In today's global marketplace, tens of millions of people have moved from being employees to being independent contractors.

We have increasingly become a culture of free agents. We come together around projects or initiatives, do our work, and then move on to something else. Access to high-speed connectivity and to wireless technologies allows us to work anywhere. We can go to an office if we want to, but it is only necessary for in-person meetings, interactions, and collaboration. And we as a society have finally embraced this. Whereas even during the last part of the Threshold Decades, people often felt they had to hide the fact that they worked from home, now in the Shift Age we are proud that we work from home. I myself work from home (or in a hotel room, or on an airplane)— and I like to say I have a ten-second commute.

This new work reality often also means that the work we do and the people with whom we do it are global in scope. Expertise, knowledge, and talent are in demand globally. As free agents with desired competencies, we can offer our services to anyone in the world who might want them, thanks to the accelerated connectedness of the planet. Project teams of independent contractors are now routinely formed using multinational and multi–time zone members.

One of the consequences of this new globally distributed workplace is that people are ever less restricted by place when it comes to earning a living. If one does not have to regularly go into a factory or office but can work from home, the opportunity for that home to be in a desired place to live increases. If home is where the work is, then the opportunity to choose where to live based upon personal preference increases.

At the same time, when place is no longer the significant conceptual reality, those economies that were protected by a nationalistic place-basedness experience loss. This has clearly been apparent in the United States, where the wage structures and costs of manufacturing ceased to be globally competitive, so those jobs and industries moved to places that were more economically efficient in the new global economy. This is painfully transitional stuff for the countries that lose. We will see the development of regions where place dictates production work and regions where the desirable places will attract those who can both work from home and leave to fly anywhere in the world their services are required. In the latter half of the book, I will suggest what the global outcomes could well look like as the global reorganization and integration completes this first historic cycle.

As I will discuss in subsequent chapters, this ability for individuals to work independently, to in a true sense become their own jobs, is part of a redefinition of what employment and the job are in the Shift Age. The concept of employment has moved from the lifelong employment of the mid-twentieth century to the serial employment of the late twentieth century to the project-by-project work of the independent contractor or free agent. Of course, there will always be jobs at institutions, corporations, and governments, but people increasingly define themselves by what they do rather than for whom they work.

## Choice and Control

We also have incredibly more individual choice in our personal lives as well. Many of the developments in the Threshold Decades have given each of us relatively unlimited choice compared to times past.

In the mid-twentieth century, it was broadcast networks that defined television. In the late twentieth century, cable started to reshape television. Now the word *television* has ceded to *video*, and the new model is one of YouTube and other video-based sites.

This explosion of choice has firmly placed control and therefore power in our hands. We have come a long way from a century ago, when Henry Ford, describing the Model T, said "People can have any color they want, as long as it is black." We have come a long way from the 1970s when, in the United States, the three broadcast networks were programmed by three people sitting in offices in Manhattan, just blocks apart from each other.

The advent of 24/7, "always on" culture means that we can shop, work, and play whenever we want to, on our own schedules. Programmable DVRs, low-cost terabyte-plus

Cloud computing is an accelerant to the move to mobile computing, as it allows people to instantly access vast amounts of data via portable devices that have limited storage. One could think of a tablet as a window to the clouds. Again, we are freed up from a place. The Cloud is always available to us, wherever we might be.

external hard drives, and instantaneous connectivity through cloud computing give us access to information and entertainment anytime, any place on almost every digital electronic device we own. We have completely customized media experiences. Hundreds of millions of people walk around with iPods and other digital players, listening to their own personal soundtracks. Compare this with the limited choice of radio stations in the last century. We have our favorite websites bookmarked on our computers, and blogs and newsletters inbound via email or RSS feeders. We see the world through the apps we select for our smartphones and tablets. We sit on the couch and use our remote controls to make second-to-second decisions about what to watch on television. We program our own media experiences rather than having someone program them for us. We are in control.

# The End of Alienation

Unlimited choice has also dealt a blow to alienation. In the decades immediately after World War II, alienation was clearly present in the developed nations. Those nations were dominated by big business and big government, mass media and mass culture, as well as tightly defined social structures and ways to dress. If you were not in step with these big entities and rigid structures, you felt alienated. Now, in the Shift Age, alienation has largely disappeared due to unlimited choice.

Accelerating connectivity allows us to find others like us anywhere around; we create and identify with "tribes" of like-minded people. We can find places and groups that we can develop affinity with rather than be alienated from. Our identities are aggregations of our choices. We determine what we like to listen to, watch, wear, or do for recreation. Ever increasingly, what we do for work and how and where we live is up to us. We no longer measure ourselves against the mass models; instead, we group ourselves around our interests and activities. The concept of conformity has lost its grip on us. We are all individuals who may choose to be like others, but being like others is no longer as socially imperative as it was just a few decades ago.

# The Micro-Micro

How will the Flow to the Individual change the world? There will be a decrease in the power of institutions and organizations. Society is being reorganized around the macro-macro (the Flow to Global) and the micro-micro (the Flow to the Individual). The smallest and largest economic units have increasing gravitational pull.

The institutions that came into existence over the last 300 years are declining in power, membership, and influence. Residual social institutions from the days of landed aristocracy or from the gilded age of robber barons have greatly declined in importance. Unions, service organizations, and the corporation itself, while all still important, are no longer as much a part of one's identity as in generations past. What one does is more important than who one works for or what one belongs to.

Media is a large institution that is experiencing the Flow to the Individual in a significant way. Mass media created in the twentieth century: newspapers, magazines, radio stations, and television stations created by media companies and sent out to the masses. Then, in the early part of the twenty-first century, non-media companies started to generate content and therefore became media companies as well. Now, in the early years of the Shift Age, content creation has moved to individuals, so now individual humans have each become media companies. Ever more content, be it written words, photographs, or videos, is being created by individuals. We have moved from few to many, to many to many, to one to all or one to one to one to one. The individual tweeting from her phone has replaced the beat reporter of newspaper from days gone by.

In fact, starting with the Threshold Decades, the mass market as a whole has been in steep decline as an influence. We deal now with an aggregation of small, targeted micromarkets. The "Long Tail" concept Chris Anderson so excellently described in his book of the same name is the new shape of the market in the digital world. Now that products are as much digital as physical, markets will and can be smaller and ever more customized. The word "fragmentation" has been used a lot in the last twenty years, but it is an old reference point, as it speaks to the fragmentation of the marketplace, which assumes a mass market. Think instead of this transition of mass to micro as a historical process that will continue and accelerate.

# The Global Individual

Ever-increasing choice, ever-increasing connectivity, ever-increasing mobility, and ever-increasing independence from institutional jobs or traditional distribution models are all part of the Flow to the Individual.

The Flow to the Individual and the Flow to the Global combine to reshape how we think of ourselves. Increasingly, we are self-articulating individuals who identify ourselves as global citizens.

Both of these flows have been, are, and will be amplified by the third force of the Shift Age: Accelerating Electronic Connectedness.

# CHAPTER FIVE

# ACCELERATING ELECTRONIC CONNECTEDNESS

The third major force of the Shift Age is the Accelerating Electronic Connectedness of the planet. It is also one of the most significant forces in the history of humanity.

The force of Accelerating Electronic Connectedness, particularly in its Internet manifestation, has been much written about and certainly widely experienced. So it can be easy to forget that it wasn't always this way.

Until the latter part of the Industrial Age, entire civilizations, societies, and countries developed largely confined to their geographic spaces. During the course of human history, there were often civilizations in the world that existed simultaneously but were not aware of each other. They could not interact, but instead experienced their entire trajectory in isolation, only later connected by historians.

This only recently began to change. Samuel Morse introduced a superior telegraph in 1837, and this new communications technology reached across the Atlantic in 1866, less than 150 years ago. The Bell Telephone Company introduced telephone service in the United States in the last twenty-five years of the nineteenth century, but it wasn't until 1956 that the transoceanic cable brought two-way telephone calls between North America and Europe. So it has been less than sixty years that we have had the experience of transatlantic two-way telephone calls. Global human communications connectivity is that recent.

Today, though, there is a simultaneity in global communications that is unprecedented. The Accelerating Electronic Connectedness eliminates time and distance from human communication, greatly contributing to the pervasive sense of speed in today's world, creating a transformational immediacy of human connectedness. This connectivity in our society is approaching a singularity—the moment when an idea moves almost simultaneously through a population.

The Occupy Wall Street phenomenon of 2011 is a recent and probably early example of what will increasingly happen. On September 17, some seventy-five people collected in Zuccotti Park in lower Manhattan. One month later, on October 15, there were tens if not hundreds of thousands of people demonstrating in more than 1,500 cities in eighty-three countries under the "Occupy" banner. A global movement in just one month!

This is something that was unimaginable until this century. And it is the force of Accelerated Electronic Connectedness that enables this to occur. Before, distance meant time for information to move, which up until the 1800s was the speed of a horse day, how far a horse could travel in a day. Compare that to today, just 200 years later, when communication is almost instantaneous. And as our electronic connectedness continues to accelerate, we will see even more change shape how we live in the Shift Age.

## Accelerating

Accelerating Electronic Connectedness is occurring at rates that twenty, fifteen, ten, or even five years ago could not be predicted, except perhaps by science fiction writers. I have personally lived with a clear example of this over the past five years, as I've studied the growth in cell phone usage.

To get a full perspective, let's step back in time a bit. Electricity was first offered as a commercial and consumer product by the California Electric Light Co. in 1879, 133 years prior to the writing of this book in 2012. The first cellular phone was commercially introduced in 1983, twenty-nine years ago, by Motorola. There will be 6 billion cell phone subscriptions in 2013, roughly 85 percent of the total global population.

Yet it is estimated that there will be approximately 1.1 billion people without electricity in their home in 2013. In other words, in 2013 the number of people who have in-home electricity, a 133-year-old consumer product, will be the same as the number of people who have cellular phones, a twenty-nine-year-old consumer product.

The disparity between the spread of electricity and that of cell phones of course is due to the huge differences between the capital-intensive supply infrastructure of electric energy and the much less expensive cellular infrastructure.

In 2007, as I was developing the concept of the Shift Age, and writing the book with that name, I was fascinated by the incredibly rapid rates of connectivity that were occurring. I had already identified Accelerating Electronic Connectedness as one of the three forces of the Shift Age, and I wanted to see and shape what it would look like going forward. A focus of this research was to try and determine what the actual trajectory of cell-phone connectivity and the number of users might be in the years ahead. So of course this led to research on what experts around the world saw coming.

Be they telephony experts, international organizations, communications companies, or technology think tanks, they all had approximately the same forecasts. In answer to the question, "When will humanity reach 3 billion cell phone users or subscribers?" the general response was sometime in 2010.

Why did they all say this? Well, it took about twenty years for humanity to go from the first commercial cell phone to the billionth. It then took only four years to get to 2 billion, in 2006. So what was the general prognostication, then? It went something like this: "Wow! A 500 percent increase in the rate of growth! That is so fast we can't imagine it growing any faster, so we will just project that linearly into the future. Let's see, it is now 2006, so we will reach 3 billion cell phone subscribers sometime during the year 2010."

Using this approach, the aggressive forecasts were that we would reach 3 billion cell phone users in early 2010 (the less aggressive suggested by the end of 2010). In addition, even the more aggressive forecasts showed it taking until 2025 to reach 5 billion cell phone users.

But as Figure 13 shows, humanity actually crossed the line of 3 billion cell phone subscribers by the end of the first quarter of 2008. This means that every day, from mid-2006 until spring 2008, there were 1.5 million new cell phone subscribers **a day.** If you recall from an earlier chart in Chapter Two, there were 700,000 cell phone subscribers in the world in 1985, **so every day in 2007 there were twice as many new cell phone users as in 1985.**

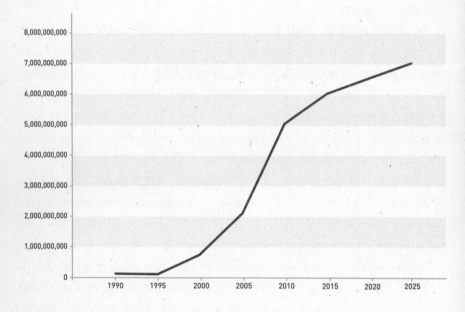

FIGURE 13. GLOBAL CELL PHONE USERS

Humanity then crossed 4 billion cell phone users in the first part of 2009, 5 billion users by the end of 2010, and 5.3 billion by the end of 2011. We are currently close to 5.6 billion. Sometime in 2013, we will reach 6 billion users.

So the reason that all projections of cell phone users have been so off until the last three years is that the rapidity of growth is unprecedented in human history. There are several reasons for this. First, the cellular infrastructure can be developed more rapidly than any previous communications infrastructure. Second, the costs of cell phones and the use of them plummeted more quickly than expected, making purchasing and using cell phones cheap very quickly. Third, the acceleration of the technological innovation in the Shift Age is unprecedented, which thus renders prior rates of change obsolete.

# The Transformation of Communication

So what does the current reality of 5.6 billion cell phone users mean? How is it changing the world we live in?

Well, if I was standing ten feet from you and used my cell phone to call your cell phone, it would probably take about five seconds for your phone to ring. If I were to call a cell phone in China, some 12,000 miles away, it might take an extra two to three seconds because of the additional satellite relay. Which means that today, the difference between calling someone ten feet away and 12,000 miles away is two seconds.

So for the first time in human history, there is no longer time or distance to limit human communication! That could not be said even ten years ago, let alone twenty-five or fifty years ago. This is a completely new human reality.

When you call someone from cell phone to cell phone, after asking "How are you doing?" and "Can you hear me okay?" one of the first things you often ask or are asked is "Where are you?" This of course is due to the fact that we move around the world and take our cell phone with us. Place has therefore also become irrelevant to human communications (except of course for the ongoing frustration of finding good cell phone reception!).

So for the first time in human history, it can be said that time, distance, and place no longer limit human communication.

Think about that! In the some 150,000 years that modern humans have lived on earth, only in the last five years has human communication been freed from the limitations of time, distance, and place. Imagine living three, two, or even one hundred years ago and trying to comprehend communication with another human being not constrained by time, distance, or place. This was not true even at the beginning of the Information Age. It would have been an incomprehensible concept. Yet it is now our reality.

This is the new reality of the Shift Age. It is a profound difference from the Information, Industrial, and Agricultural Ages, and will be one of the major factors shaping our future.

# The Internet

In Chapter Two we saw that it was in the second half of the Threshold Decades that the Internet and usage of it took off. We have lived in an Internet world for some seventeen years. We have lived in a high-speed Internet world for less than ten years. We have lived in a high-speed wireless world for less than five years. Now, the "we" I am referring to is the developed countries of the world, with the United States initially leading the way. As the developing countries of the world come online, the growth in the number of Internet users is explosive. As Figure 14 shows, we are at the early stage of Internet usage.

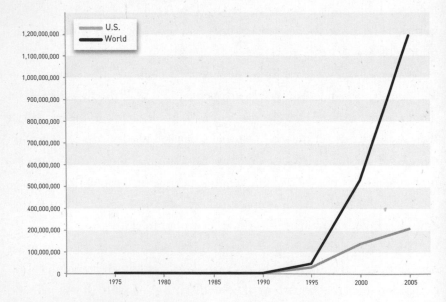

FIGURE 14. NUMBER OF INTERNET USERS IN THE U.S. AND WORLD

To use the United States as an example of a developed country, Figure 15 shows both how recent high-speed Internet is and how pervasive it has now become.

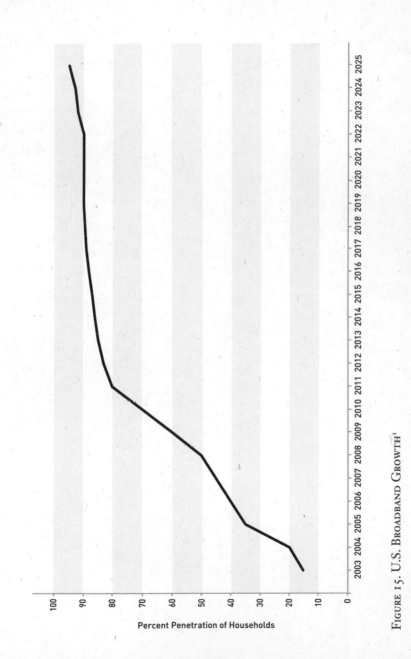

Figure 15. U.S. Broadband Growth[1]

Percent Penetration of Households

As more users come online, and bandwidth and high-speed access grow, we also face an explosion in the amount of data that will course through the Internet backbones of the planet.

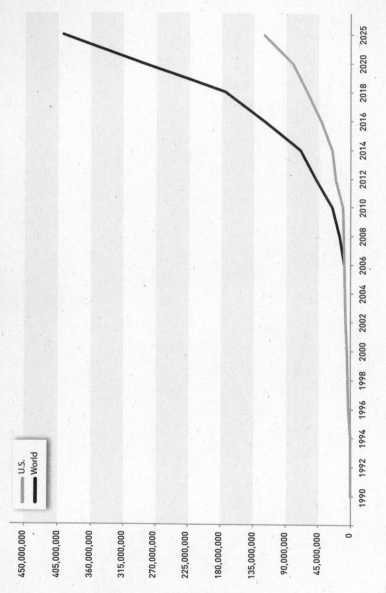

FIGURE 16. TRAFFIC ON INTERNET BACKBONES[2]

So, we have ever more people using high-speed Internet connections, creating ever more data. This has created an entire new reality that did not exist twenty years ago or even ten years ago.

We now have two realities we live in: real or physical reality and new screen reality.

# The Two Realities

Prior to the development of communication technologies of the last 200 years, the Concept of Place was an overriding reality of human life. Where one lived largely determined one's life—other places could not be experienced without often lengthy and arduous travel. This meant that the Concept of Place was a dominant reality and one's life was largely defined by what one did and experienced in that place. "Reality" meant physical reality.

Even during the explosive growth of communications technologies such as the telegraph, telephone, radio, and television from the 1830s through the 1970s, one had to be in a specific place to communicate with another place. The telegraph office gave way to the telephone at home (even in many developed countries outside the United States, having a telephone in the home was a luxury and not universal until years after World War II), and at the office, both connected to the wall. The radio was big and in the home. The television set was big and in the living room. The experienced reality was still about places with these electric devices anchored in them. So one lived in a place, was largely defined by that place, and had connectivity to the world through these place-based appliances.

No longer.

As Figure 15 shows, we now live in a broadband world. We live *in* the world of connectivity. This new broadband world shows up on screens, be they large flat screens, computer screens, laptop screens, tablet screens, or smartphone screens.

This screen reality can be every bit as compelling as the physical reality that we physically inhabit. Do we not all "check our screens" with close to addictive regularity? Isn't how a teenager is perceived at night on Facebook every bit as important to her as how she is seen in school the next day?

This connectedness, happening at the speed of light via fiber optics, is creating an entire new place: the neurosphere. Our physical reality exists in the biosphere—the thin surface of the planet where life exists. But this new, rapidly growing neurosphere is the electronic extension of our collective neurological activity. It is a pulsing cyber-repository of humanity's creative brainpower, its knowledge, history, culture, social interactions, entertainment, and commerce. This is a global village vastly more comprehensive and interconnected than Marshall McLuhan could ever have envisioned when he coined the phrase "electric village" more than forty years ago. We now live in a two-reality world: the physical reality in which we live and the neurosphere reality of the screen that connects us to everything and everyone else on the planet.

The Shift Age is the first time that humanity has experienced these two realities. As we will see in later, the unfolding truth is that these two realities will develop at significantly different evolutionary rates. This will cause incredible transformation of physical reality and of human consciousness.

# The Evisceration of Ignorance

This accelerated connectedness and dual reality will have profound effects on our culture and politics. These effects will be most evident in an evisceration of ignorance.

Throughout history, kings, dictators, leaders of religions, and leaders of sects ruled, to some degree, by keeping people ignorant. Populations had to accept what they were told by those that ruled them, as there was no other option. Before Gutenberg, there wasn't even a strong way to transmit information among people across distances. Even after Gutenberg invented the moveable-type press, the resulting communications were limited. Even up into the twentieth century, when the world noticeably sped up, closed societies such as the Soviet Union, China, and North Korea could simply block or jam incoming printed or electric communications from outside the country. The phrase "ignorance is bliss" was a lived reality.

But now, due to the Accelerating Electronic Connectedness of the planet, such ignorance is practically impossible. A compelling example of this change has been occurring in the Middle East.

Now, I am generally optimistic and excited about the coming transformations of the Shift Age. This also comes through when I speak to audiences. And often, in the time period of 2007–2009, I was questioned about this optimism. People would often point to the dictatorships and radical Islam and dictatorial Islamic states. My response was always the same. I said that within three to five years there would be upheavals in most dictatorships and in many Islamic states because of this Accelerating Electronic Connectedness. That the fundamental force of the Shift Age would force those closed societies to open up. I didn't know to call it "Arab Spring," as of course I had no idea it would happen in the spring, but I was clear that it would happen.

The two common denominators of all of the countries that experienced upheaval and revolution during the Arab Spring were these:

> » Electronic connectedness—Facebook and Twitter were the weapons of revolution
> » Forty-five to fifty-five percent of the populations of these countries were under the age of twenty-five

The second factor is important to note as well. The Millennial and Digital Native generations are more tech savvy and more connected than any prior generation in history. They are using the inventions created in the last two decades to actually change history and transform the world. I will write of them in future chapters here.

The Arab Spring is just one of many events to come where the Accelerating Electronic Connectedness of humanity will change the world. Simply put, this third fundamental force of the Shift Age is one of the most significant forces and occurrences in recorded history. It is changing our reality and our consciousness faster than any before it. It is not only a force in and of itself, it also amplifies and accelerates the Flow to Global and the Flow to the Individual.

When 80 percent of humanity has the capability to connect with each other, any time, from almost anywhere, it amplifies the Flow to Global, as we are now connected for the first time in history. The Accelerating Connectedness of the planet has provided the technological connectivity for humanity to be as one, all connected to each other.

When any one of us can put out a message or develop content that can be shared—often at the speed of light—with up to 80 percent of humanity, we each have potential new powers of influence no longer limited by place, class, wealth, or institutional power. So this Accelerating Electronic Connectedness places power in the hands of individuals, thus amplifying the Flow to the Individual.

It is this force that is providing and will provide the technological underpinnings of all the changes we are now experiencing as we enter the Shift Age.

# PART 3 | THE TRANSFORMATION DECADE 2010–2020

# INTRODUCTION

**transformation**

1: the act or process of transforming.

2: the state of being transformed.

3: change in form, appearance, nature, or character.

—Merriam-Webster Online Dictionary

Remember back in 1999, when the dominant question asked in the latter part of the year was "What are you going to do and where are you going to be on New Year's Eve?"

The general thinking was that we were crossing into the new millennium, since all four digits were going to change. Now we know that the new millennium actually started in 2001, but as humans we seem to look at dates as though they were on an odometer. Because the 1999–2000 New Year's Eve had all four digits rolling over, like a noteworthy mileage event on one's odometer, the significance felt great. Thus, in practice around the world, it became the Millennial transition.

The same thing happened toward the end of 2009. Mainstream media spent the latter part of December 2009 wondering out loud what the decade just ending had actually been called and what we might call this new decade. So, on the interesting digital date of 01-01-10, I published a column naming this "new" decade "The Transformation Decade."

The huge and immediate reaction to this column gave me pause to reflect even more deeply on the naming of this decade and the word *transformation*. Seeing how much the three fundamental flows of the Shift Age were changing the world, the word *transformation* seemed to be a perfect description of what will happen in the decade of 2010–2020, when humanity and most of its institutions will transform. This means that companies, institutions of any kind, and the way we think will all experience a change in form, appearance, nature, or character—or will no longer exist or have much strength going forward.

The Transformation Decade is the first full, delineated decade of the Shift Age. By 2020, it will be clear to humanity that we are living in the Shift Age, but for now, the world is just coming to grips with this transformation.

# An Inflection Point in History

We are living in and through one of the most transformative times in human history.

Think about the fact that in 2012, when this book is being written, we are just a bit more than 1 percent through this new millennium. The last time that statement could have been true was the year 1012, when it was the middle of the Dark Ages in Europe and the Vikings ruled the seas.

But the transformation we are experiencing today is even more profound than the one in 1012. We are actually experiencing four major changes:

> » We are living in a new millennium
> » We are living in a new century
> » We have entered a new Age, the Shift Age
> » We have entered a new decade, the Transformation Decade

All of this aligned at one period of time—what an amazing inflection point in history.

As I wrote earlier, the speed of change has accelerated to the point where we live in an environment of change. I think that most readers would agree that the speed of change is at least ten times faster than it was in 1012. If you accept that premise, then the amount of change that humanity has experienced in the last 1,000 years will be the amount of change we experience in the next 100!

Upon reflection, that idea is easy to embrace. The majority of change in the past 1,000 years occurred in the last 400 years, and most of the change of that time occurred in the last 100 years. The rate of invention, discovery, scientific inquiry, and technological innovation has exploded in the past 100 years, and even more so since the beginning of the Threshold Decades in 1985. Thus, I actually believe that the speed of change is 100 times faster than it was in 1012. If this is true, then the amount of change humanity has experienced in the last 1,000 years could be equal to the amount we experience in the next ten!

No matter which rate you go with, it is amazing that sometime between the next ten and 100 years, we will experience the amount of change we have experienced in the last millennium. Another way of saying this is that, if a lifetime is fifty years, then all the change of humanity's last twenty lifetimes could well be replicated in the lifetime of those now alive.

Just stop a minute and really think about what that means. Think about what the world looked like in 1012 compared to today. There were no real nation-states. There was almost universal illiteracy. Little was known about the Planet Earth—let alone its place in the universe, which was a concept yet to be held in human minds. It was called the "Dark Ages" for a reason. Compare the change between then and now, and imagine that amount of change taking place in the next ten to 100 years. No wonder we feel disoriented and question what lies ahead!

We are indeed living at an inflection point in human history and evolution.

Another way to look at the Shift Age as a key inflection point in history is through the filter of fundamental changes in personal communication. As we saw in the last chapter, the Accelerating Electronic Connectedness of the planet has forever changed our perception of time, distance, and place. This is a communications inflection point. And it is preceded by a history of age shifts triggered by changes in communications.

An "age shift" often seems to coincide with major changes in portable communication media. The time it takes between the changes is roughly shrinking by a factor of ten. Take a look at the timeline on page 73.

The prospect of continuing this pace boggles the mind. Will there be a time soon when, within a period of six months, we have another hyper-leap in human communication? Perhaps not right now, but in the future, it could be probable.

Another way to look at this progression is to accept that we have now arrived at the true moment of presence, the immediacy of communication with no time, distance, or place. We have arrived at a seminal moment in the history of human communication. We stand at the culmination of millennia of the evolutionary process of communication that is without precedent. This will have powerful and profound consequences for every industry and field in the coming decades. (We will look at some of these in depth in Part Four.)

We have entered the Shift Age, a time when almost everything is in some rate of shift. The Shift Age will be looked back upon as having ushered in the greatest amount of change up to this point in human history.

People sometimes speak of "going back" to the way things were, or trying to hold on to the way "it used to be." This is not possible. Reality is changing ever faster, and we need to understand it to keep up.

# The Power of the Transformation Decade

The Transformation Decade is the first full decade of this new age, and it will manifest the changes that will greatly alter humanity's evolutionary trajectory. In the following section, we will look at the change that is happening now and that is on the way in this Transformation Decade. Knowledge is power—knowing what this decade will bring will give you the ability to operate not from a place of fear, but from a powerful understanding of the opportunities this future brings.

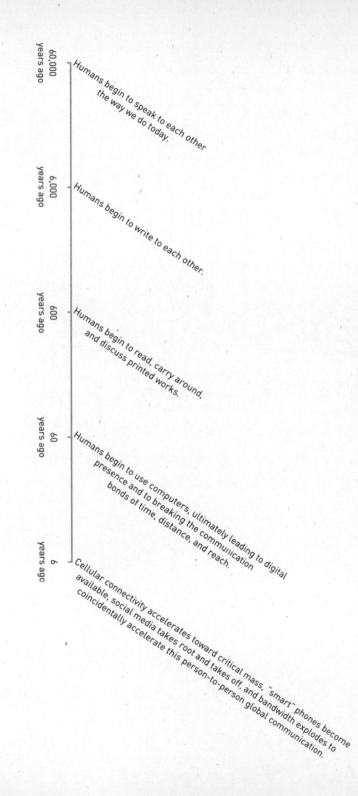

60,000 years ago — Humans begin to speak to each other the way we do today.

6,000 years ago — Humans begin to write to each other.

600 years ago — Humans begin to read, carry around, and discuss printed works.

60 years ago — Humans begin to use computers, ultimately leading to digital presence and to breaking the communication bonds of time, distance, and reach.

6 years ago — Cellular connectivity accelerates toward critical mass, "smart" phones become available, social media takes root and takes off, and bandwidth explodes to coincidentally accelerate this person-to-person global communication.

# CHAPTER SIX

# THE FIRST DECADE OF TWENTY-FIRST-CENTURY THOUGHT

The Transformation Decade, 2010–2020, is obviously the second decade of the twenty-first century. However, due to the legacy thinking now collapsing in the world, this second decade is actually the first real decade of twenty-first-century thought.

What do I mean by twenty-first-century thought? Let's tackle that question by asking a different one:

> » What do you think of when you hear the phrase "twentieth century?"
>> » The century of science?
>> » The century of World War?
>> » The American century?

Well, whichever of these you think of, they all really began with World War I and the years 1914–1918.

This first industrialized war ushered the world into the twentieth century. It was the time that the maps of Europe and of the Middle East, for the rest of the twentieth century, were largely set. The Russian Revolution initiated the historically short but significant era of communism. Aviation and deadly weapons were developed for World War I, beginning the massive buildup of military might of the century. Einstein's Theory of General Relativity was published in 1916. And the United States went from being an isolationist country to one of the leading powers in the world.

So, when we look back at the trajectory of history of the last century from the vantage point of 2012, we can see it largely began in the second decade of the twentieth century. It was this decade that began the major story lines of the century.

It did not happen in the decade before. Think about the decade 1900–1910. It was the end of Victorian England. The United States was still largely agricultural and did not yet have forty-eight states. The 400 families of the social register of New York, descended from early settlers and the families of the robber-baron age, tightly ruled society. The map of Europe still looked much as it had decades earlier. It wasn't until the next decade, and the end of World War I, that everyone realized that the world had changed.

Now think about the decade 2000–2010. It was a flat decade from an economic point of view; the developed countries ended up in 2010 pretty much where they were in 2000. But in hindsight, the evidence of the coming changes can be seen everywhere.

All of a sudden, things seemed to no longer work. The reorganizational recession of 2007–2012 destroyed the idea of ongoing growth of the late twentieth century that had been embedded in these countries. Industries that were dominant in the latter quarter of the twentieth century were disrupted and were surprised when this disruption occurred.

To use Thomas Friedman's metaphor, this was the decade when the world was flattened due to several dynamics. Yet, while the world flattened, the thinking of the prior century still held sway. The emerging global economy was fully noticed, yet it was perceived as a changed competitive landscape where rules were changing, not the beginning of the fundamental shift to globalism that it was.

Debt, and the use of credit—which had expanded in an unprecedented way in the last half of the twentieth century—finally hit the wall. It was as though a comfortable, known way of looking at finance simply disintegrated before our eyes. What had been a good, acceptable pathway to the realization of dreams became an unfathomable nightmare.

The global reign of terrorism, led by such groups as Al Qaeda, that began in the 1990s reached its zenith in the 2000–2010 decade and, by the time of Osama Bin Laden's death in late 2011, was significantly receding outside the Middle East and parts of Africa. Yet Cold War perceptions of the geopolitical landscape still held sway in many governments. This made them look like stubborn boulders in a rapid flowing river of change.

Another concept in public discussion was whether corporations and institutions were was "too big to fail." Perhaps a better question would have been, and is, "Are corporations a twentieth-century business model that no longer works in the twenty-first century?"

The widespread human reaction was, "What is going on? Why is our reality changing? Why is the worldview we are holding no longer in sync with what is going on? I don't like this, so I want to go back to the time when my thinking was aligned with the reality I understood."

So the first decade of the twenty-first century was when the models, constructs, and worldviews so deeply held in the twentieth century were under attack but not fully understood. The developed countries of the world, which had largely become developed during the twentieth century, carried their developed ways of thinking and ways of acting into the twenty-first century. The corporations, though one of the faster-moving segments of society, were still being run on management ideas that quite quickly became out of sync with the rapidly changing world of the Shift Age.

We are now only beginning to understand this change in our global society. The Transformation Decade of 2010–2020, then, is when much of what was accepted in the last two ages and in the last century will be dramatically altered by the forces of the Shift Age. When I say that this is the first real decade of twenty-first century thought, I mean that 100 years from now, historians will look back at the decade we now live in, 2010–2020, as the decade that began the major story lines of the twenty-first century. Thinking about almost everything will undergo a change in nature, shape, form, or character.

# CHAPTER SEVEN

# THE COLLAPSE OF LEGACY THINKING

The Transformation Decade, 2010–2020, will be a time when an incredible amount of change will occur. Most of humanity's institutions and ways of thinking will change their nature, character, form, or shape. A fundamental reason that this will happen is that legacy thinking will fall away, collapse, or be rendered obsolete.

What do I mean by "legacy thinking"? Legacy thinking is viewing the present and future through thoughts from the past. A simple metaphor for this would be the act of rowing a boat. You are looking back to where you have been with your back facing where you are going. You are backing into the future, looking at the past.

We all do this. We all have core ideas and beliefs that we hold because we were taught them, were told to believe them, or discovered them on our own. We carry them with us and use them as filters to view the world, to solve problems, to live our lives, and to consider the future.

Take a minute and think about thoughts you have around almost anything, and you will see that you are confining your view of the present or of the world because of legacy thinking from your past.

> » Do you still hold on to beliefs, taught to you in childhood, that you are superior because of the religion that you were raised in, the race that you are, or the country or part of the country in which you were raised?

- » Do you follow a political party because it is the one your parents supported?
- » Do you think that having a detailed business plan, a physical office, and a lot of money are essential to the starting of a business?
- » Do you root for a sports team because of where you live or because it is the one your parents rooted for?
- » Do you hold onto a philosophical view of the world because twenty years ago it fit your perception of the world for you at that age?
- » Do you hold on to definitions of decades ago and assume they are true today? For example, what does it mean to be conservative or liberal in politics?
- » Is your definition of a "good time" the same now as it was fifteen years ago?
- » Do you think that work and play must be separate places in your life because of some early "truisms" that may not be true?
- » Do you hold on to some brand as part of your identity because at one time you thought it was cool or aspirational?
- » Do you consider someone a friend because they used to be, but perhaps no longer are?
- » When you go to the grocery store, do you follow the same pattern of shopping you did twenty years ago?
- » Do you define a relationship as one that is face-to-face only?
- » Have you ever declined to try something new because you "know what you like"?

Many of these examples to some degree relate to our own sense of our social self and identity. Yes, it is good to have a strong sense of identity and sense of self, but if your social self-definition is the same it was five, ten, or twenty years ago, might not you be holding onto legacy thinking due either to a need for security or to a lack of curiosity?

Legacy thinking is often why it is hard to see change, especially now, because we are living in the present through the filters of the past. Only when the change becomes personal do we understand the change. And then there is a conflict: either you have to accept that your legacy thinking is no longer valid, or you hold on for a more secure and comfortable view of the world. That is why people get so upset by change—it threatens their point of view or worldview.

Take a moment to think about your own thoughts and how you use them to evaluate and see the world around you. Are you looking at what is going on in 2012 through the filter of concepts or thoughts that you accepted as valid for the first time years or even decades ago?

If you are older than thirty-five, then your early formative years and perhaps much of your adult life have been in the twentieth century, learning the best ways to navigate that century. But this means that you are viewing this new century through the lens of the last century. And most of us are doing this. Humanity, particularly in the developed countries of the world, has powered into this new century with all kinds of fixed ideas that lead not to clarity and change, but to resistance and risk.

To see an example of how legacy thinking can hold us back in the midst of change, we only have to look back to last century. The Industrial Age thinking of the early and middle parts of the century came up against the changed landscape of the Information Age. As the Information Age took over, we were surprised to be confronted with vibrant cities becoming parts of a "rust belt." How did this happen? Through outdated thoughts and assumptions that things would continue the way they have been.

Up to the 1970s, it was almost an axiom that high inflation, slow economic growth, and high unemployment never happened simultaneously. How could it? Industrial Age thinking was clear on this; high unemployment would necessarily hold down inflation. But in the 1970s, economic reality turned this thinking upside down. A word—"stagflation"—had to be created to describe this phenomenon that didn't fit the economists' worldview. Entire regions of the United States underwent profound, devastating collapse in the early years of the Information Age, as the legacy thinking of the Industrial Age ruled politics and economic policy. The

Another example of legacy thinking was the American automobile industry as it entered the 1970s. It was an axiom that Americans wanted big cars and wanted them new every few years. Planned obsolescence was integral to the marketing of automobiles and other large purchases. Then all of a sudden the game changed. People in the Middle East quadrupled the price of oil, and people in Japan produced automobiles less expensively that were small, didn't look sexy, and used much less gasoline. Politicians and union members prompted people to take sledgehammers to imported small cars—a nice Stone Age touch—and set up tariffs to protect an industry that was already out of touch with global trends and changes in consumer thinking.

Instead of trying to win by adapting, American politicians protected the status quo that had been so triumphant in the 1950s and 1960s. As a young boy growing up in Chicago, it was always an incredible sight to drive east with my parents through Gary and Hammond, Indiana, and see by day, or even more spectacularly at night, the world's center of steel production belching fire as thousands of tons of steel were created for industry. As an adult, I drove this same route and saw only a toxic wasteland in what had been one of the most formidable industrial landscapes in the world. This death occurred as humanity moved from the Industrial Age to the Information Age and as American political and business leaders—if not citizen consumers—still thought the country was both largely in control and leading the economic thinking of the world.

economic thinking and subsequent policies of the 1950s, a great decade for America's ascendant economic power, still held sway well into the 1970s, with unforeseen and catastrophic consequences.

In the 1950s, the developed countries of the world, led by the United States, held that manufacturing was the center of the economy, as the consumer society needed things to buy and things were manufactured. Everything was based in physical reality. Countries were thought of as independent entities with independent tastes and business models.

Legacy thinking also delayed the West from seeing how the world would change at the end of the twentieth century. After living for almost fifty years in a cold war with the Eastern Bloc, the West turned inward once that war had been won. It didn't see that a global economy was dead ahead, with all the resulting disruption in domestic economies as hundreds of millions of new worker/consumers came online. An "us versus them" thinking had so ruled western cultures that the victory of democracy over communism kept the West from realizing the new risk from a virulent, non–nation-state enemy—terrorism.

So why do we continue to hold on to legacy thinking, even if just the recent past shows us how harmful it can be in a time of change?

Most people have an organized way to look at the world. They build this view through experience, reading, or learning from people they respect. Once in the brain, this becomes fixed as one's "valid" view of the world. In order to see the future, you have to break that view.

As a futurist, I "live" in the future, but most of us don't. At any moment, there are people embracing the future and seeing change, while others are steeped in the past. Change, evolutionary change, and the loss of legacy thinking don't happen to all of us at once but move through human society across time. But in the Shift Age, the amount of time from inception of an idea to its being generally accepted is getting ever shorter. As the great contemporary science fiction writer William Gibson famously said: "The future is here, it is just not evenly distributed." So, a lot of the future is already here, and as the speed of change increases, the rate at which we lose our legacy thinking is going to increase rapidly.

We can all see and feel that the thought patterns and structural ways of thinking we learned in the past no longer seem to work. That is why so much of the world, particularly the political and governmental world, seems to be locked down and unable to adapt to or solve the new emerging issues of the twenty-first century.

To lead in the Shift Age, especially in this Transformation Decade, you will need to abandon your own legacy thinking. Such phrases as "This is the way it is done," "This is the way our industry works," or "We are on top, we are the greatest/we are the biggest/we have the largest market share" are some of the most dangerous thoughts to think—ever, let alone in the Shift Age.

And you have to watch situations for where legacy thinking is poised to collapse in your field and in the world. In 2012, two years into the Transformation Decade, I see an incredible amount of legacy thinking about to fall away. Simply put, the Transformation Decade will be the time when the legacy thought of the twentieth century and the Information and Industrial Ages will give way to the new ways of thinking:

» The way we look at the world
» The way we perceive ourselves and our roles in the world
» What we do for a living and how we do it
» The global economy and how it affects the economies of the nation-states
» How we communicate
» Health care and medicine and how we look at health
» Education at all levels

Everything.

## Areas of Legacy Thinking Collapse

What follows is a partial list of areas where there will be a collapse of legacy thinking during the Transformation Decade. Some of these areas are already experiencing the collapse of legacy thought. Others will occur in the years before 2020.

Recall that we are in a constant state of change. Some people are ahead of the curve and see some or most of it, while, at the same time, there are people who cannot see any of it because they are seeing through their thinking from the past.

If any of what follows strikes you as improbable or even ridiculous, please pause to evaluate what thoughts or points of view you are holding on to that make you resist accepting these ideas. If you feel resistance, please do some introspection to get to the root of that resistance and why you feel it or think it. Is it due to something someone—some political party, some leader, some family member, or some friend—told you? If you are resistant to embracing these changes that are and will be occurring, you should at least understand why.

This is a quick list of coming transformations. What these transformations will lead to will be discussed in more depth in Part Four.

## THE NATION-STATE

We have now entered the global stage of human evolution. This means that we are moving toward more global integration economically, socially, culturally, and ultimately politically. This Flow to Global means that the function and independence of nation-states around the world must and will change.

As discussed earlier in Part Two, economics usually is the initial driver or impetus for change. Anyone reading this book has already accepted, to some degree, the reality of the new global economy. We now see, all around us, how culture has gone global via the unprecedented connectivity described earlier. Politics is now starting in that direction, initially via issue-based situations such as climate change, the connectivity of the financial sector, and the questionable future of some currencies.

The nation-state will not go away, but its independence and separateness from the rest of the world is over. The Transformation Decade will be looked back upon as the time when the several-century-long apotheosis of the nation-state ended and the Flow to Global began.

## GOVERNMENTAL STRUCTURES AND POLITICAL PARTIES

As this book is being written in 2012, it is quite clear that governments and politicians are not leading. The people are leading.

Governments around the world are largely constructed with Industrial Age models: hierarchical bureaucracies populated with long-term employees who have little or no urgency to move quickly or reinvent themselves. They are the slowest moving segment of society.

Perhaps the best metaphor for the relative speeds with which social institutions change was set forth by the great futurists Alvin and Heidi Toffler in their book *Revolutionary Wealth*. They suggested the metaphor of a cop parked on the side of the highway pointing his radar gun at the oncoming traffic. "On the highway there are nine cars, each representing a major institution in America. Each car travels at a speed that matches that institution's actual rate of change." Then they go on to list, from fastest to slowest, the rates of speed, providing descriptions on each one. The following list summarizes the institutions and their relative rates of speed, as the Tofflers saw it in 2006.

| 100 mph | The company |
| 90 mph | Civil society, including NGOs |
| 60 mph | The American family |
| 30 mph | Unions |
| 25 mph | Government bureaucracies and regulatory agencies |
| 10 mph | The American school system |
| 5 mph | IGOs, or international or intergovernmental agencies |
| 3 mph | Political structures in developed countries (Congress, the presidency, political parties) |
| 1 mph | The law and the courts |

It is clear that the various forms of government are moving more slowly than the rest of society. Through time, this has led to a distinct disconnect between what is new, dynamic, innovative, and hyperconnected in society and the governments that preside over the populations hurtling into the future. Since change has now become environmental and everything is in some rate of shift, we are fast approaching a time when there will be a globally held perception that governments around the world no longer solve problems, but *are* the problem.

As this book is being written, people in many countries believe that the political system no longer works. In the United States, the perception is that politics and democracy are corrupted by money, that they move too slowly, that they are holding the country back, and that the two-party system is broken. In other countries, such as Mexico, France, Great Britain, Germany, and India, the ball of leadership and dominance is tossed back and forth between political parties that have ruled the roost since World War II. In China, the legacy of the Communist Party still dramatically clamps down on the ability of citizens to live as they want. This frustration with governments is occurring around the world. The governments are seen as stuck in the nationalistic, regional, political-spectrum thinking of centuries gone by. Governments, particularly national governments, seem to be the single greatest impediment to moving forward, to embracing change, to living in the twenty-first century.

Speed-of-light connectivity among billions of us, the Flow to Global, and the urgent problems humanity faces will soon bring about a change in the nature, character, shape, or form of nation-state governments. Think about the "memes to movements" mentioned earlier, with Occupy Wall Street being an early example. Seemingly instantaneous, connected uprisings will alter how we think about the ways we are governed and in fact alter the law.

This is the future of how we interact with our governments. Political parties, outdated government institutions, and bureaucracies will be significantly altered in the Transformation Decade. The future will bring new parties, new memes, and new assertions of the power of individuals rising up together.

An example from 2012 in the United States is the SOPA legislation. In the traditional, slow, lobbyist-led process, companies spent money on persuading Congress to pass a bill that would severely limit or censor the Internet. This bill took months to move through this ancient, deliberative process, slowly approaching a vote. In the final month of the process, Internet-based companies such as Google, Wikipedia, and others rang the alarm bells throughout the connected populace who, seemingly in a matter of weeks, rose up loudly and successfully worked to block passage of this bill. The connectivity of the Internet, the power of the individual, and the rapid speed which an idea can course through society trumped the centuries-old, process-bound Senate with stunning force.

## HEALTH CARE AND MEDICINE

The Transformation Decade will perhaps be the single most significant decade in the history of health care and medicine. As my coauthor

Jonathan Fleece and I wrote in *The New Health Age: The Future of Health Care in America*, we are in a New Health Age of amazing transformation in how we think about, deliver, and pay for health care.

The history of health care is quite recent. The Band-Aid is less than 100 years old, antibiotics are less than seventy-five years old, and modern medicine is only about 150 years old. So we often forget how dynamic change in health care is.

In this decade, we will see medicine transformed by ongoing breakthroughs in genetics, medical devices, stem cell utilization, and neuroscience. Globally, health care will move from the current "pound of cure" model to that of "ounce of prevention." The phrase "health care" will be replaced by the phrase "health management" as we move to preventative health from treatment of sickness. Legacy thinking about life expectancy will be challenged as we approach living to 100. The current way we speak of and handle death will dramatically change as we move to controlling how and where we die. Economically, health care will move into the rest of the global economy where free-market competition, open competition on pricing, and electronic connectivity will bring us transparency and patient-centric control at a level previously unheard of.

## EDUCATION AT ALL LEVELS

As this book is being written, transformation is coursing through education around the world. K–12 education is undergoing the single greatest transformation since *Sputnik* triggered the math, science, and engineering educational explosion in 1957 in the United States.

As the Toffler radar-gun metaphor shows, the education system moves at one-tenth the speed of the company. No wonder there is a skills and knowledge gap! Given that this has been going on for decades, educational institutions and processes are so far behind that transformation is the only way they can survive and be relevant around the world.

In *Shift Ed: A Call to Action for Transforming Education*, a book I coauthored with Jeff Cobb, we made it clear that "reform" is an old word, no longer relevant. Transformation is the only way. The way we think about the school year and the school day, the way students can move as quickly as they want through subject matter, and the connected technology increasingly available to all will largely alter the thinking and therefore the landscape of K–12 education in the United States and around the world.

The Khan Academy and the Gates Foundation, along with hundreds of transformation-oriented school superintendents, principals, and teachers, are creating new ways of learning, assessment, and curriculum. In 2012, in the United States, we are entering a phase of transition from the legacy failures of the past to the new dynamic successes of the future.

Higher education as well will undergo transformation between now and 2020. The 500-year-old university model will change more in the next ten years than it has in the last 100. The economics are unsustainable, the outcomes are questionable, and the insularity and inefficiencies intolerable. The institutional constructs so long in place are in early-stage collapse. How higher education looked in 2010 will feel antiquated by 2020.

> High-speed connectivity is allowing the creation of online and video courses by such great universities as Harvard, MIT, and Duke to be taken, viewed, and consumed by tens and even hundreds of thousands of people. Higher education is leaping from the ivy-walled confines of campuses to computers everywhere.

## GENERATIONS

A changing of the generational guard is and will be one of the most significant developments of the Transformation Decade. The Millennials and Digital Natives are distinctly different from the Gen Xers and Baby Boomers that preceded them. As they age and assume positions of authority and influence, they will lead transformation across the board.

The Millennials, the twenty-somethings who have come of age in this new millennium, have entered the workplace with great impact, impatience, and purpose. The work place has been, is, and will be for a few more years a battleground between the Baby Boomer bosses and business owners and the incoming Millennials.

The Digital Natives, those that are from the high school class of 2012 and younger, are even distinctly different from their older Millennial brothers and sisters. Why call them Digital Natives?

> » They are the first of all generations to be born into the digital and information-overloaded world.
> » Anyone over the age of thirty in 2012 is a digital immigrant; they came to the new digital world as a teenager or adult.
> » This means that, unlike those over thirty today, Digital Natives even have a hard time understanding why their elders feel overloaded with information.

This generation will have a profound effect across the board.

## ENERGY AND ENERGY USE

Humanity has spent 200 years consuming fossil fuels, and it will continue to do so. However, fossil fuels as a percentage of energy generated will start to decline significantly in the Transformation Decade. The legacy thinking that is deeply embedded around energy will fall away. The thinking will become more systemic. It is clear now that the conversation on energy must and will move from which sources of energy we use to a more holistic, systemic look at the integration of *all* forms of energy into a cohesive, reality-acknowledging global construct.

We now know that our long, unbridled embrace of fossil fuel has consequences for Planet Earth. The thinking about energy in the Transformation Decade will move from industry specific and nation specific to global. All forms of energy, old and new, will move toward a blended whole that acknowledges the economic, climatic, and social realities now facing humanity.

These are just a few of the significant areas of human endeavor that will undergo significant collapse of legacy thinking. We now take a quick look at some concepts, ideas, and overarching patterns of thought that will affect many of these and other areas of human activity in the Transformation Decade and the Shift Age.

Some of the areas of transformation mentioned previously and the following ideas will be explored in the following chapter, and all will be looked at with greater depth in Part Four.

# Ideas and Concepts That Will Take on New Meaning and Acceptance in This Decade

So you can see, as humanity undergoes a change in nature, shape, form, or character in this Transformation Decade, old ways of thinking will fall away and be complemented or replaced by new ways of thinking. Here is a short list of some ideas ascendant in this decade. These are large concepts and ideas that will emerge to replace the legacy thinking still in place.

» It becomes clear that growth and sustainable growth are and must become ever more congruent.

» While the twentieth century was very much a left-brain century, the twenty-first century will be a right-brain century.

» Design is ascendant: of objects, systems, ecosystems, mega-cities, and lives.

» National governments will no longer be able to operate at their historically slow speeds. The Industrial Age constructs that still largely shape governments today will give way to the more net-oriented and connected forms of the Shift Age.

» Migration will change in shape. Once a permanent, one-time act, migration will become widespread and temporary, as tens of millions of people migrate from place to place for work and life, supported by the ever Accelerating Electronic Connectedness of humanity.

» The dual realities of physical reality and screen reality will evolve at distinctly different rates, with the latter morphing much more rapidly. This will lead to a developing shift in consciousness through screen reality that will become disjointed both from and well in advance of physical reality. This will be a significant separation new to the human experience.

» The concept of "place" will be changed forever. Place will move from a consciousness- and life-restricted reality to more of a temporary idea. Having two different realities leads to two different senses of place.

» The thinking of the planet as "Spaceship Earth," a whole, interactive, integrated entity, becomes largely embedded in humanity.

As you now see, we are living in a decade when so much legacy thinking of the past is falling and will fall away. In this Transformation Decade, many of the accepted ways of thinking and ideas of the Industrial Age, the Information Age, and the twentieth century will lose their power, truth, validity, and therefore their hold on how we think and how we look at the world. As we are confronted with the new realities, issues, and problems of the Shift Age and, longer term, the twenty-first century, this collapse of legacy thinking is coming just in time.

Let us now take a look at some trends and forecasts flowing from this collapse.

# CHAPTER EIGHT

# GENERAL TRENDS AND FORECASTS

As a futurist, I am always asked to predict trends and make forecasts—and I do. People want some sense of guidance or context for what may lay ahead, particularly in times of uncertainty and anxiety, certainly a description of our time since 2007. But one-sentence forecasts do not give context or depth; they are just statements.

In the last chapter, I highlighted a sampling of areas that are undergoing and will undergo significant change due to the collapse of legacy thinking occurring in the Transformation Decade. I ended with a short list of predictive statements that, in varying degrees, describe causes for some of this collapse. I would now like to go into greater depth on some of those forecasts on that short list.

These are forecasts and trends for this decade 2010–2020. In Part Four, I will look longer term and examine where these current trends will ultimately take us in the Shift Age.

So, if you are someone for whom a futurist has a purpose because he can give you forecasts to consider and perhaps guide you for a few years, this is your chapter!

What are some of the major general trends and forecasts of the Transformation Decade, 2010–2020?

- » The Concept of Place continues to be eviscerated
- » A major generational shift takes root

» Biology and technology merge ever more
» Spaceship Earth becomes a more widely held mindset
» Creativity is a dominant value
» Globalism ascends, nationalism declines
» Governments shake loose many of their Industrial Age structures
» Energy moves into its systemic stage

All of these trends will be looked at within specific areas of society and human endeavor in Part Four. Some of these trends affect humanity widely, others more narrowly.

# The Concept of Place Continues to Be Eviscerated

Recall that with 5.6 billion cell phone users there is no longer any time, distance, or place limiting human communication. We can call 80 percent of humanity any time, from any place, and distance adds only seconds at best. The Accelerating Electronic Connectedness of humanity and the planet has eviscerated and will continue to eviscerate one of the most formative ideas of humanity, the Concept of Place.

Think about how through most of humanity's history, place was a significant and defining concept. Until the 1800s, a horse day defined speed of travel and communication. Until well into the Industrial Age, the place where one lived not only defined oneself but even defined the knowledge one had. Great civilizations, even expansive ones such as the Roman Empire, were locked into a sense of place that had a restrictive view. "All roads lead to Rome"—what about the oceans and the other continents?

As discussed in Chapter Five, great civilizations that existed simultaneously didn't even know of each other's existence due to distances between places. It wasn't until the last 100 years that large numbers of people could transcend place with communications. The telegraph, telephone, radio, television, communications satellites, and, most recently, cell phones and the Internet all sped up our ability to communicate, made the world "smaller," and created social and national interactions in real time that would have been unfathomable throughout most of history.

We can now stay plugged in to events around the world as they happen. We can now chat with family members or business associates on the other side of the world, live on video. We can fly halfway around the world in a day. We can work from almost anywhere. We can be plugged in via our screen reality in such a way that a lot of our physical reality is trumped.

One hundred years ago it would be unthinkable to work in one part of a country and live much of the time in another, either connected or with speed-of-sound travel. I know many people who now do that all the time.

We will see in Chapter Twenty-Four that this new reality is affecting vast sections of humanity in profound ways.

# A Major Generational Shift Takes Root

One of the most significant dynamics in the world today and for the rest of the Transformation Decade is the historic generational shift that is taking place. The two generations that are and will be initiating fundamental change globally are the Millennials and Digital Natives.

Much has been written about the Millenials. They have been endlessly analyzed, criticized, and judged by generations older than they. But it is always a trap to have one generation analyze another, as generational viewpoints are often deeply embedded in the analysis.

What is clear is that the Millennial Generation is changing the world. Their connectedness, their collaborative ways of engagement, their impatience and need for constant feedback, and their civic-mindedness are creating a new way of looking at and living and working in this new world of the Shift Age.

They are challenging twentieth-century legacy thinking in this new century. They look around at the catastrophic global recession and rightly point the finger at the older generations that created it. They exist around the world and can therefore be a generation that collectively can change the world as they can come together and say, "Sorry, you Gen Xers and Baby Boomers have created an economic mess and a developing environmental nightmare, and we aren't buying into it. Time for change."

It is the twenty-something Millennials around the world that will be assuming positions of power this decade. They will be inventing entirely new ways of thinking and doing things. The waves of innovation today, particularly in the technology and communications sectors, are being led by this incredibly dynamic generation.

**Millenials:**

» Are over age twenty in 2012
» Are innovating technology and communication
» Will invent new patterns, structures, and ways of thinking

**Digital Natives:**

» Are under twenty in 2012
» Were born into the information-overloaded and hyperconnected world
» Will lead to new level of consciousness

The Digital Natives are the first generation born into the digital landscape. It is their native land. This generation has never known a world without cell phones, the Internet, mobile computing devices, and social media. Think about a three-year-old in 2012 who is using an iPad and interacting with the world through that portal. How is that child going to show up as a twenty-year-old in 2029?

Another way of thinking about the Digital Native generation is that they are the first generation born into the information-overloaded world in which we live. Ask a ten-year-old how they are handling information overload and they will look at you wondering what you are talking about. So this generation has no problem whatsoever with the hyperconnected world we now live in. Their total comfort in, and utilization of, the Accelerating Electronic Connectedness of humanity is creating an entirely different consciousness, one radically different from their elders. While the Millennials will be creating new social, economic, and political web-oriented patterns and structures, the Digital Natives will be leading us into a new level of consciousness in the decades ahead.

We will take a deeper look into these two generations in Chapter Fourteen.

# Biology and Technology Merge Ever More

Entering the twenty-first century, most of humanity largely thought about biology and technology as distinctly separate. Biology was about living things, and technology was about inanimate things created by man. Now, in the Transformation Decade, the line between the two is dissolving. We are seeing biology move into technology and technology move into historically biological areas.

Nanotechnology, and the ability to manufacture at the cellular level, is opening up incredible new areas of scientific endeavor that will redefine medicine, computing, and almost every area of society. It seems as though almost every month there is some nanotechnology breakthrough that will "revolutionize" this or that segment of science.

The world of medicine is experiencing an infusion of technology that is changing our view of health and longevity. The world of computing is experiencing the first-ever introduction of biology into its core of chip development. The new age of computing will involve biological chips (now in development); the new age of health will involve technological devices implanted in the body.

This new merging of biology and technology will, in the next decade, make us think anew about long-held definitions. Centuries-old concepts of what is life and the creation of life will be challenged by this development. We stand at the threshold of redefinition of technology, biology, and life itself.

# Spaceship Earth Becomes a More Widely Held Mindset

"There are no passengers on Spaceship Earth. We are all crew."

—Marshall McLuhan

When McLuhan wrote these words more than four decades ago, they were prophetic and not widely understood. Today they speak to a rapidly growing awareness of the finiteness of Planet Earth. Humanity is experiencing the reality of climate change, disruptive weather, environmental degradation, the depletion of life in the oceans, and species extinction.

The space exploration race and adventures of the last century have left us no closer to other worlds to inhabit. We have pushed the pause button on expanding the manned exploration of space. We increasingly are seeing Planet Earth as the precious place it is. It is our place, our only place, and we are collectively beginning to see that we must change our ways to preserve it.

As we will see in Part Four, we have entered The Earth Century.

Simply put, the twenty-first century is the Earth Century. We can no longer celebrate Earth Day, month, or year, but now must look at all issues environmental and planetary through the lens of this being the Earth Century. What humanity does collectively and when we do it in the twenty-first century will be one of the most significant decisions for the future of humanity and our existence on Planet Earth.

# Creativity Is a Dominant Value

The twentieth century has often been called the century of science. The number of inventions and technological and scientific breakthroughs of the last 100 years rival all those of the prior millennia.

The launch of Sputnik in 1957 ushered in a U.S.-led infusion of science, technology, engineering, and math in educational systems around the world. Educators refer to this as the STEM curriculum. Left-brain thinking prevailed. It served the world well as the Industrial Age moved into the Information Age.

In the twenty-first century and the Shift Age, though, creativity is the ascendant quality. Humanity must now take all that we have learned, invented, and discovered through science and left-brain logical thinking, and redeploy it with creative, right-brain thinking.

Creativity is and will be the top quality corporations seek in this new age. In fact, *Fortune* magazine, the magazine for corporate America and the designator of the Fortune 500 companies, announced in 2009 that the "CEO of the Decade," for the first ten years of the twenty-first century, was Steve Jobs. Jobs was not an engineer or a finance type. He was a designer, a very creative and demanding visionary.

Creativity is needed to look at things in new ways, to "think outside the box," to find new paradigms, and to create new designs, forms, systems, businesses, and products. Almost every area of human endeavor is now facing the need to have creative thinking and ideas to help create new solutions to old problems that linger and to work on the new problems emerging. We have an urgent need to think differently as humanity.

Simply put, if the twentieth century was a left-brain century, the twenty-first century will be a right-brain century.

## Globalism Ascends, Nationalism Declines

In the Shift Age, we live in a global economy. The problems we will have are global in scope. The connectivity we have is global in scope. The way we communicate transcends national borders. So we will most likely develop global policy and political and governmental entities for the first time in the next decade.

The nation-state, the highest-level structure created by humanity to date, will now start to be superseded by the Flow to Global. Nation-states will, of course, continue to exist and will continue to drive much of the world's thinking and politics. It is just that they are in the process of becoming ever less relevant to solving the global problems we now face.

New global entities will come into being, initially issue driven. Once these entities are in place, the nation-states will evolve, or devolve, more into the actual functioning of the state, the safety of the citizens, the utilization of the land, and to the general well-being of the citizens. National governments will increasingly "protect" their legacy cultures of history, now resurrected for holidays and in museums.

This ascent of globalism and decline of nationalism will both be accelerated and countered by the next major trend below.

## Governments Shake Loose Many of Their Industrial-Age Structures

The majority of nation-state governments today were created in the Industrial Age, and even those created after have been largely patterned on the Industrial Age ones. Lower-level governments, states, provinces, cities, and counties have largely mimicked the hierarchical structures of national governments. So, the overwhelming majority of governments today are largely structured as Industrial-Age hierarchical bureaucracies.

This is about to change dramatically.

One way to look at this is through the radar-gun metaphor of the Tofflers that was mentioned earlier. Since governmental structures and agencies have been moving at much slower rates than the rest of society, a huge gap has developed between the slow-moving governments and the faster-moving citizenry that they govern. It is time for catch-up.

As corporations, particularly U.S. corporations, realized in the 1980s and 1990s, there is a lot of savings to be gained by eliminating layers of management and making organizations ever more flat. In this century, corporate productivity has increased dramatically because of utilization of technology, particularly communications and mobile technologies. The excruciating pressure of debt and deficits will now bring these dynamics to government. Financial pressures will now flatten and shrink governments around the world.

People are becoming ever closer globally, global constructs are ascendant, and the speed of change is now environmental. Governments currently often keep people apart, are constructed on national orientation, and move very slowly, but that is all about to change. The sheer power of transformation that is driving most everything else will now come to government.

# Energy Moves into Its Systemic Stage

How humanity thinks about and uses energy will be profoundly different in the Shift Age and the twenty-first century than it was in the Industrial and Information Ages and the twentieth century.

For most of humanity's history, wood was a primary fuel. Then, over the last 200 years, it was replaced by fossil fuels. Now, as we move into the Earth Century, there is much discussion about all the alternative and renewable sources of energy that must be scaled up due to economic and climate reasons.

You will recall that in the Threshold Decades, western science "proved" that everything was energy, a confirmation of eastern thought that all was connected and that all was energy. So, if everything is energy, then there are many more sources of this energy to be developed, utilized, and deployed.

It is clear that energy thinking can no longer be about which source of energy is better or cleaner or cheaper or more renewable. It is much more about an "all of the above" approach in the next few decades. There will be continued use of fossil fuels. There will be rapidly scaled-up renewable sources of energy, such as wind and solar. There will be dramatically increased conservation and energy efficiency.

Much of the history of energy has been about discovery, location, cost, and cut-throat commercial competition. In the last few decades, geopolitical and environmental considerations have become front and center in the thinking and talking about energy. There have been heated and endless arguments over which source of energy is better and for what reasons. All of this past will now move toward a more integrated systemic view of energy. We will start to look at the planet and all of humanity as a single source of and a single market for energy.

The Flow to Global and the Spaceship Earth thinking mentioned previously point toward this integrated global way of thinking that makes this systemic approach to the entire subject of energy a reality.

# A Shift in Every Field

This chapter has provided you with some quick, high-level takes on dominant trends of the Transformation Decade, 2010–2020. These trends will continue to have lingering effects beyond 2020. We now move on to see both how they might shape major areas of society and to delve into other trends, forces, and defining issues of the Shift Age.

# PART 4 | THE FUTURE OF THE SHIFT AGE

# INTRODUCTION

In Part Four, we will look at the future by first focusing on some large concepts and contexts of the Shift Age, followed by a close look at particular segments of society and humanity.

In Chapters Two–Four, we looked at the three dominant forces of the Shift Age: the Flow to Global, the Flow to the Individual, and Accelerating Electronic Connectedness. These three forces are driving several big ideas that are initiating massive change now, and will have largely reshaped our world by the year 2025.

One clear difference between the Information Age and the Shift Age is content and context. The true cliché of the Information Age was "content is king." The reality of the Shift Age is "context is king." Entering the Shift Age, we live in an increasingly contextual world. I have selected the five contexts I think have the greatest impact and influence.

## THE FIVE MAJOR UNDERLYING CONTEXTS OF THE SHIFT AGE

1. The Earth Century
2. The need to retrofit the twentieth century
3. The permanent change in the Concept of Place
4. The merging of biology and technology
5. The move toward an evolutionary shift in human consciousness

So now let us begin by taking a look at these five contexts, and then explore what much of society will look like in the years and decades ahead. Some of the areas of the future we will explore are Shift Age Generations, Education, Technology, Energy, Brands and Marketing, the future of the Nation-State and Power—all areas that will have transformational change.

It's time to Enter the Shift Age and our collective future.

# CHAPTER NINE

# THE EARTH CENTURY

The first large context through which we must view the Shift Age is that the twenty-first century is the Earth Century.

Humanity has entered the twenty-first century with a rapidly growing awareness that it is having a significant effect on Earth. Environmental awareness, climate change, drought, record heat, and extreme weather are all showing us that something dire is going on with our planet. And there is increasing evidence that we are causing this adverse effect on Earth. This understanding will shape a great deal of the change we experience in the Shift Age.

## A Quick Look Back

Earth Day was first celebrated in 1970. This event, to some degree, was a result of the question Stewart Brand asked in the late 1960s: "Why haven't we seen a picture of the whole earth?" Then we had the classic "earthrise" photo taken from an Apollo spacecraft in 1968. What we all saw stunned us. There, in the midst of infinite blackness, was this beautiful blue and green planet we call home. It looked so finite, and indeed fragile, that we understood the name Spaceship Earth. Alone in the midst of infinite space was our home, our only home.

This photo arguably launched the environmental movement, with Earth Day 1970 being a formal beginning. This environmental mindset took a while to take off, however.

Then, in the 1990s and into this century, environmental consciousness exploded. As a Baby Boomer parent, I marveled at the commitment my young son had to recycling. It showed me that a new generation was being raised with embedded environmental awareness that was far more fully developed than any I had known prior to the first Earth Day.

When Al Gore came out with his *Inconvenient Truth* presentation and film in 2006, it was clear that this awareness had gone beyond the new younger generation, the hardcore environmental movement, and a growing body of scientists. While this event, and to some degree Mr. Gore himself, triggered a backlash, the direction was clear. All of us, to a greater or lesser degree, were now living in both the conversation about man's effect on Earth and that developing reality.

## Helping to Shape the Thinking

In the first two to three years of my blog, I wrote a lot about energy, alternative energy, climate change, and other environmental issues. I became known early on as a "thought shaper" regarding such topics, which led to invitations to attend conferences and to speak. A few years later, when blogs had truly gone mainstream, I started to get lots of inbound solicitations to write about this new "green" product or that new LEED certified building, to review a new book on some environmental subject, or perhaps to interview a scientist or environmental entrepreneur. In other words, I had gotten on the larger PR radar as someone with an audience who should be pitched stories and interviews.

A *thought shaper* is a person who creates, shapes and drives the perspectives and discussions surrounding various ideas and thoughts.

In 2011, all of this simply became too much. Though Earth Day was in late April, I started to get pitched story ideas for columns around Earth Day starting in early March. By early April there were half a dozen inbound solicitations every day. All of these folks seemed to think that their product was a great green product and that Earth Day was a great marketing hook or tent pole. Earth Day was perceived as a marketing event. This prompted a strong reaction in me.

In my Earth Day column that year, I spoke of my disgust with this view and said that Earth Day was not a marketing event, that it was no longer an Earth Day, an Earth Month, or even an Earth Year. While Earth Decade was somewhat more palatable, I basically said that we all had to think differently and that what we really needed to do was to think of the twenty-first century as the Earth Century, thereby coining a phrase I have used ever since. In that column I wrote:

> The twenty-first century will be the Earth Century. It will be during this century that humanity faces the reality of whether it wants to destroy itself and much of what exists on this magnificent planet or not. Assuming we make essential course corrections, future historians will write about the Earth Century as a turning point in human history.
>
> So folks, stop getting excited about Earth Day. Retire that thinking and refocus on the next ninety years of the Earth Century.

# The Current Reality

This is where we are. There are more than 7 billion of us alive today. There are tens of millions of people entering the middle class around the world each year. We are still overwhelmingly dependent on fossil fuels, and that reality will only change slowly.

We now feel a finiteness about Earth that has largely not been felt before. We are living in a time of historic animal and plant extinction. Oceanic animal populations have declined dramatically. Extreme weather and natural disasters are increasing. Water is becoming the next big resource issue for humanity.

The idea of looking at our planet as Spaceship Earth is being ever more understood and embraced. An increasing number of humanity now sees the truth in the aforementioned quote from McLuhan that "There are no passengers on Spaceship Earth. We are all crew." We have no place else to go; we are here. This is it.

> The Shift Age is and will be the age when humanity alters its sense in relation to our planet. This goes way beyond what we think of as the environmentalism of today. It is a much more long-term stewardship point of view. All of our previous history has been about growth, economic growth, and use of the planet's resources for our immediate needs. The earth seemed to be unlimited in its space, resources, and ability to absorb whatever humanity did. No longer.

The integration of East meeting West mentioned earlier has given us a developing sense of integration, that the earth is an integrated, highly intelligent living system. As the great scientist James Lovelock wrote in his several books about Gaia, earth functions as a single organism. In the 1970s and 1980s, his theory quickly moved from the environmental fringes to mainstream thinking. It did and does have eminent scientists who disagree with it, so it is disputed science, but it is one point of view. In recent years, Lovelock has written with despair and despondency that a tipping point of disruption due to human endeavors might have already been passed, and that the next century could be one of global environmental catastrophe, resulting in mass migrations. He has recently stated that this might happen later than he first thought, but that it most likely would happen by 2100. I think that this is a considered possibility, one that will become a central discussion in the Shift Age.

# The Anthropocene Era

As we think about the Earth Century, we must also remember that we are now fully in the Anthropocene Era. Loosely translated, this means we are in the age of humanity.

There is some scientific discussion as to when this Anthropocene Era began. Some scientists think that it began some 10,000 years ago, when man put down roots and the Agricultural Age began. Others contend that it began with the Industrial Age 300 years ago, while many think it really began in the last twenty-five years of the twentieth century, when carbon emissions dramatically increased. Regardless, we are now in it and will be in it for a long time.

The Anthropocene Era is a very good way to start thinking about all things having to do with the environment, energy, and all areas of humanity's relationship with our beautiful planetary home. We are clearly the dominant species on the planet, and we are certainly intrusive and manipulative in our relationship with the planet. So our species is now the single greatest determinant to the biosphere of Earth. The future of the biosphere of Planet Earth is now, to a great degree, in our hands.

*Anthropocene Era* was a term made popular by Paul Crutzen, a Nobel Prize-winning Dutch scientist at the beginning of this century. He was thinking that what is generally regarded as the current epoch, the Holocene Era, was no longer valid, as so much has changed in the 12,000-some years since it was acknowledged to have begun.

In Greek, *Anthro* means human, so *Anthropocene* means the epoch of humanity. Thus we have now entered the epoch of Earth when humanity is the single most profound influence upon the Earth. As ice was the dominant influence in the Ice Age, humanity is now the dominant force on Earth in the Age of Humanity.

We must integrate the Anthropocene concept into our daily thoughts. I know this sounds like a stretch, but most things can be best understood when made personal. One way is for everyone who has yet to have a grandchild but expects or hopes to have one to think about that grandchild in the future. In the Earth Century, what we do this decade will affect the lives of those in decades ahead. Do you care if your yet-to-be-born grandchild cannot live a natural life, at least in the way we describe it today? Does it matter to you if your grandchild is part of a generation that looks back to your generation as the one that took no action, the consequences of which might be a highly compromised way to live in the 2050s and beyond?

At this juncture the conversation about humanity's effect on Earth is a largely negative one, highlighting all the things our species does that have adverse consequences, debated only by the degree of the effect. In the Shift Age, though, I believe that the thinking will become much more proactive—not just what we can do to slow down harmful practices and trends, but what we might be able to do, create, and invent that could positively change or reverse these threatening trends.

As we will discuss at length in the chapter on energy, humankind must now start to think holistically and systemically, relative to our relationship to Earth. That is why the Gaia concept is worth holding. We all know now that a coal-powered electric plant anywhere in the world can affect the air somewhere else in the world. We know now that a tsunami-damaged nuclear plant in Japan can make tuna in the Pacific radioactive, and debris from it can wash up on North American shores. So the Earth Century is the first century when humanity will live with the daily reality that whatever we do, individually and collectively, will have an effect, positive or negative, on the planet we share.

Living in the Earth Century is a Shift Age reality. The longer we remain passengers and not crew, the more urgent these creations and inventions become. Welcome to the Shift Age!

CHAPTER TEN

# RETROFITTING THE TWENTIETH CENTURY

A nother large context by which the Shift Age will be framed relates to how we view, and live with, the effects of the twentieth century.

## A Time-Lapse Photographic Sequence of Change

It could easily be argued that more change and alteration occurred in the twentieth century than in the prior 150,000 years of modern human life. The twentieth century, more than any other 100-year period in history, altered the landscape of the planet.

Imagine a theoretical time-lapse photographic sequence where, at the beginning of each century since 1000, there was a panoramic photograph taken of the region where you live. Now flip through those images in order. There may or may not have been noticeable change through the first nine photographs through 1800, depending on where you live. But no matter the place, by the tenth photograph, in 1900, there was probably some noticeable change from the prior one.

Now imagine that theoretical photograph from 1900 of almost any inhabited place on the six continents and compare it to the one taken in 2000. Wow!

What is in that 2000 photograph that was absent in the one from 1900? A partial list:

- » Roads and highways for automobiles
- » Airports
- » Skyscrapers
- » Pipelines
- » Suburbia
- » Motorized and electric public transport
- » Shopping centers
- » Office and industrial parks
- » Telephone lines
- » Electrical lines
- » Radio, TV, and satellite towers, antennas, and dishes
- » Gas stations and fast-food restaurants
- » Widespread use of concrete
- » Smog and pollution

None of the above existed or was very prevalent in 1900. If you look at this list, then look around whatever country you are in right now, you will see that most of what dominates our places now is from the twentieth century.

Not only that, but the twentieth century, as discussed earlier, was the first century in which the global population quadrupled. So if you combine the physical changes above with the quadrupling of the population, it is clear that the physical reality of our society and economy today is largely a product of the twentieth century. Never before has humanity entered a century so fully defined physically by the prior one.

As a futurist, I see this as a highly limiting and confining reality. We live in a world largely created last century. The spaces we inhabit, the transportation that moves us around, the energy and the utilities we use all contain us in "twentieth century-ness."

# The Need to Let Go of the Twentieth Century

The first problem with this confinement is the concept of legacy thinking discussed in Chapter Seven. When our entire environmental surroundings are of the twentieth century, it makes it ever so much harder to think twenty-first-century thoughts. In a sense, our surroundings cocoon us into accepting the twentieth-century foundation as *the* reality and then support the continued ways of thinking that came into existence with this reality.

The second, more significant problem is that, as all 7 billion of us enter the Earth Century, much of all this twentieth-century stuff is not sustainable, integrated, intelligent, or smart.

If you question that last sentence, pause and imagine 2100. Do you think that, in that year, your grandchildren or great-grandchildren will get the gas tank filled up to go to the mall to shop for stuff? Do you think that they will get into a car by themselves to drive one to two hours to go to a place of work at the same time everyone else does? Of course not! But because that is the world that surrounds us, we continue to have our thinking shaped by the twentieth century.

In fact, we are now living in a dually perceived reality. While we live in the twenty-first century, we seem to hold—most people very strongly—to the "way things are" as what is real. Much of our daily lives has been habituated to this twentieth-century reality. There isn't anyone alive today who doesn't look at that preceding list of twentieth-century creations and see it as the reality they have known. We simply accept what we have known all or most of our lives as reality. And why not? Acceptance of something is, to some degree, acquiescence to it. The impetus to change, to see something that doesn't yet exist, to imagine a different order of things, or a different way of thinking about any topic, is ever so much more difficult when one is cocooned in rooms, buildings, rhythms, and deeply ingrained thought patterns of the past. In this acceptance we shut off the thinking of how things might change because, well, this is reality.

But at the same time, most of us also recognize that we are moving into a different time. In the Transformation Decade, we are beginning to change "the nature, shape, form, and character" of reality as defined in the last century. What this means is that, finally, our thinking is becoming more of this century than the last one.

As this continues, we will move from the dual reality to one focused on the reality of the Shift Age. Thinking precedes action. Change reorients thinking. Actions we are now taking come from this new Transformation Decade thinking, and the incredible amount of change we have experienced in the past few years is also prompting rapidly morphing views of the world and our future.

This is being driven by another duality we live with. In Chapter Five, we looked at the fact that we now have two realities we have to manage and live in: physical reality and new screen reality. They are clearly developing at very different rates of change. Screen reality is in an almost constant state of transformation. Physical reality, twentieth-century reality, is changing much more slowly. In fact, much of the change in this physical reality is being triggered by screen reality and how it alters how we do and think about things. Why do I need to go to the mall when I can buy almost anything from my tablet? Why do I need to go to the office when I can work more efficiently, and with less interruption and no travel time, from home?

So here we are, more than 10 percent into the twenty-first century, deeply entrenched into physical and mental realities of the twentieth century. Change is happening, thinking is rapidly changing, and screen reality is becoming ever more important, disruptive, and accelerative. The new global problems of the Earth Century are pressing in upon us as we remain settled into the physical reality of the last century. Many of us, particularly those of us who embrace change and understand the dynamics of the Shift Age, feel the crush and conflict between the legacy landscape we all live in and the urgent need to find new ways to live, think, and recast the past.

What do we need to do?

# Retrofit the Twentieth Century

At any time prior in history, new inventions and new things were simply created without significant restrictions from past inventions. Railroads were simply laid over the stagecoach paths, and the country roads that worked for horses and buggies became paved to handle automobiles. And there was plenty of space for new places and things to develop.

The issue we have today is the predominance of all the twentieth-century physical constructs that dominate the world. Think about the view when you travel by plane. When you fly into any large city or megalopolis such as New York, Los Angeles, or São Paulo, the approach to the airport is over an almost endless amount of urban sprawl. The often polluted atmosphere is a hazy brown or grey. This is the urban landscape of the twentieth century.

We can't simply start anew with new structures, transportation systems, and cities, leaving what exists behind. There is simply no room when the landscape is covered with these twentieth-century constructs.

Simply put, for the first time in the history of humanity we don't have a blank canvas on which to paint a new picture. Painting and creation of the new has to be infused back into the old. We must develop the vision of the twenty-first century, then turn and face the landscape dealt us by the twentieth century and retrofit it.

> » How do we retrofit the internal combustion engine infrastructure for the coming new forms of transportation?
>
> » How do we take relic constructions such as big box stores, outdated shopping centers, and empty or redundant strip malls and retrofit them for the future?
>
> » How do we take the existing vast energy-wasteful construction, built before energy became expensive and climate change became real, and retrofit it to reflect the realities of the Earth Century?
>
> » How do we retrofit huge factories and shipyards that have lost all semblance of economic viability?

» How do we retrofit old, inefficient, and crumbling transportation, energy, and communications grids?

» How do we rethink our land use to more intelligently integrate humanity, with all its needs, with the planet and its finiteness?

» How do we do all of this when the developed countries of the world are living in a fiscally restrained social and political environment that is a hangover from the last century?

These are all difficult questions. And this is compounded by the fact that we have exhausted our financial resources and political will creating what we now need to change.

I do not have the political or economic answers to these questions. I do know that, in the Shift Age, answering the larger question of how to successfully retrofit the twentieth century is critical. The first step is to realize this reality and to hold this concept in mind. As more of us understand the need to retrofit, the answers will start to bubble up, and a rapidly growing percentage of humanity can start to coalesce around the priorities needed to succeed.

The good news is that the legacy thinking of the past century is falling away in the Transformation Decade. The filters of acceptance of twentieth century "reality" are falling away as more people see that much is broken, our direction is wrong, and thinking must change. Screen reality is leading us away from the patterns and behavior of the primarily physical reality of the past. Cracks are clear, out-of-date institutions are failing, and new generations are coming into society with profoundly different ways of thinking and interacting than the generations responsible for what needs to be changed.

The new view of humanity in the Shift Age is well on its way. The thinking inside the constructs is changing, and that will lead to the changing of the constructs.

As for retrofitting the twentieth century, the **what** is becoming more clear. The **how** is beginning to be discussed. There is developing urgency around the **when**. The **who** is all of us. (And the **where** of course is our planet.)

Retrofitting the twentieth century will be a signature effort of the Shift Age as almost everything is now in relative rates of shift. Historians in the year 2100 will look back on the 2010–2020 decade as when this retrofitting began in earnest.

Just in time.

# CHAPTER ELEVEN

# THE CONCEPT OF PLACE HAS CHANGED FOREVER

I n Chapter Eight, we explored the Concept of Place. The next significant context of the Shift Age is the evisceration of that.

## The History of Place

Throughout history, humanity has been deeply connected to the Concept of Place. We are physical beings, after all, and place is a physical concept, so this makes sense. Place, perhaps more than almost any other idea, has shaped human thinking, behavior, and consciousness.

The Concept of Place really began to take root when the Agricultural Age began some 10,000 years ago. We stopped moving for food and decided to stay in one place and grow it. This not only initiated a new age, it created the idea that people are of a place and live in that place.

This, of course, ultimately led to the creation of civilization. Every great civilization that quickly comes to mind has developed since the beginning of the Agricultural Age. Civilization was the creation of societies that were place based. Societies in the desert were different from those in the mountains. Those near the Equator were different from those in the northern latitudes.

Place was a foundation of civilization, but it was also a limitation. As discussed earlier, for most of history, civilizations existed in isolation. They developed, matured, and usually declined all in one place.

These civilizations benefited and developed their true identities in place. (For example, the essence of Greece and the Greeks defined that ancient society, as the Roman Empire defined what "Roman" or "Italian" meant then and since.) For the most part, civilizations evolved on their own—in isolation. The decline in these civilizations could in part be attributed to their relative isolation and the absence of any interaction and integration with other advanced societies, interaction that might have introduced new dynamics that might have rejuvenated the civilization in decline.

The first expansion of place began with empires. Empires, such as the Roman and Ottoman empires and much later the Spanish, Portuguese, and British empires, began to connect to places beyond the home country. The British Empire was really the first global empire on which the "sun never set." Empires exported culture to the colonies on which they imposed their will. This remained the main force of exporting place until technology took hold. In fact, the beginning of place-shrinking technologies such as the telegraph, radio, telephone, and television signaled the end of the colonial era.

So all of human history has, to a great degree, been defined by place: a sense of place, the uniqueness of place, the specialness of place, a commonality of place, and the shaping that specific places supply.

Today that is still largely the case. There are many different types of place-based societies we identify with today.

Nationalism creates a unity around a place concept: a country. This is perhaps the largest place-based identity with real resonance that exists today.

Regionalism creates a unity around place within a country. In the United States, we are tied to our states, cities, and towns and relish the social aspects that come from these, such as where we went to school, the work that we do, and the sports teams we root for. In Canada, there is a great sense of province.

This Concept of Place is integral to our daily lives. Why does someone root for Manchester United, the Toronto Maple Leafs, or the Boston Red Sox? Well, in large part they probably either live or lived in the city or region where the team is. Much of who we are comes from where we were born, where we grew up, where we attended college, and where we work. Place is a defining concept that shapes all our lives more than we might acknowledge.

## The Concept of Place Is Being Eviscerated

But now, in the Shift Age, one of the key limitations of the Concept of Place has ended. Place is no longer a restriction on our ability to communicate at will with people in any other place. While it may be decades or perhaps centuries before a "beam me up, Scotty" transportation device exists to physically transport us across places, we now have the historically unprecedented ability to transcend place when we communicate.

In Chapter Five, we discussed the Accelerating Electronic Connectedness of the planet, one of the three forces of the Shift Age. This force is not only connecting us all in ways never before experienced, it is also eviscerating the Concept of Place. As of this writing, there are more than 7 billion of us, and 5.6 billion have a cell phone of some sort. This near-ubiquity creates the reality that there is no longer any time, distance, or place limiting human communication.

> Accelerating Electronic Connectedness eliminates time and distance from human communication, greatly contributing to the pervasive sense of speed in today's world, creating a transformational immediacy of human connectedness.

> We have spent 150,000 years on Earth as modern humans. Only in the last 200 years have we had any type of communication that bridged distance and place with relative immediacy. Only in the last three years have we been able to completely transcend place in communications.

We now have the potential to talk or text to any one of the 5.6 billion other humans who have a cell phone, regardless of where they are or what time it is. Due to the Accelerating Electronic Connectedness of humanity, we can also access information, news, videos, sports, and movies wherever we are. Sixty years ago the only way to access a movie was to go to a place called a theater. Until the advent and widespread availability of high-speed wireless Internet connectivity in the last few years, we had to be in our home or a theater to watch a movie. Now we can watch it on a bus or in a coffee shop.

We are wherever we are and can communicate with anyone else wherever they are. To many of us, this has quickly become the new reality, which dulls us to how incredibly profound a change this truly is.

On a higher level, if you contemplate the Flow to Global and the Flow to the Individual within this context, you can see how powerful these forces are in the redefinition of place. As individuals, we are connected regardless of place, so right now we have the power to exercise our individual power on a global scale. This reality simply did not exist until the Shift Age.

This is occurring in the Shift Age, when almost everything is undergoing significant shift. Place-based or place-influenced thought, around for centuries, is now beginning to be untethered. What will this mean as we enter the Shift Age?

Place will be less about who we are and more where we are—now. We now have the choice to let place define us as opposed to not having that choice.

"Where are you from?" moves to "Who are you here?" *Here* becomes the place, wherever here is. You are never away from home if you are electronically connected. You just might not be physically at home.

## Screen Reality Changes Place to Space

Part of this developing reality is that there is a new place that is "no-place": the Neurosphere; the synaptic, pulsating, ever-expanding, ever more in-the-cloud cyberspace.

This is where the beginnings of the separation between screen reality and physical reality start. We are losing the need to be any place, as long as we are connected. This connectivity frees us from the "placeness" of physical reality.

> **Cyberspace, not cyberplace.** This may well be the first "no-place" space ever inhabited by humanity.

Until the Shift Age there has never been this screen reality, which is fundamentally different from physical reality. Sure, since television gained market penetration in the mid-twentieth century, and the PC in the latter part of the century, there have been screens, but those screens were either one-way or contained and separate. The early-stage Internet at the end of the Information Age did initiate slow interactivity and provided us with a view into what interactivity might provide, but it was not until the last few years that interactive connectivity both went high speed and became totally mobile. It is these two coincidental developments that ended the relevance of place to human communication.

We now have a rapidly morphing screen reality that is spatial. We all accept the word *cyberspace* (thank you, William Gibson) as "where we go through our screens." We know intuitively it is not a place but a space. Further, we know that this space can be plugged into or "jacked into" from anywhere. We know that, once in this space, we can interact with anyone and any entity or source.

This is going to lead to a profound alteration in both consciousness and how we relate to physical place. Just imagine for a moment that you are sitting with someone from the past, telling them that there is a space you regularly go to, that doesn't physically exist, but where you can "be" with your friends, learn about anything in the world, or buy anything from anywhere in the world at any time it is convenient for you. They would not, could not, understand this space, except perhaps in the totally abstract sense. What might be at best a very limited abstract sense of this space, is, for you and all of us, an actual place we go every day, an actual experience we have every day.

This is a radical change in spatial consciousness. To daily enter a spatial reality—screen reality—that is other than physical reality is creating an evolutionary shift in how humanity relates to place. We are often so into this screen reality, this cyberspace, and the gadgets that are the portals to this space that we lose sight, or even awareness, of how unprecedentedly transformative this all is. Is a fish conscious that it is swimming in water?

A whole new space in which to live, a space that has no correlation to the physical place that has defined, shaped, and limited human thought and consciousness until the Shift Age. So the Concept of Place has changed forever. How much more it will change makes one wonder.

## Utopia?

The word *utopia* comes from Sir Thomas More and the Greek language, where it means "no place." So if the Concept of Place is changing and becoming less important, could that mean that we are moving toward a utopia? At the time of the ancient Greek civilization it was impossible to think of no-place, since everything exists in a place. Since "perfection, an ideal place" did not exist, the word *utopia* was created to describe the non-place ideal.

Now, if there is no longer any time, distance, or place connected with human communication, then have we have arrived at Utopia, at least in communications? Does this mean that in the Shift Age humanity might begin to experience Utopia outside communications? It is worth holding the possibility of that in our thinking about the future. It might be ours to create, or at least move towards, in this Earth Century.

Welcome to the first beginnings of Utopia. We are now here. The real question is where we go and what we do that might further expand our no-placeness, our Utopia?

Or, as one of my intellectual heroes, R. Buckminster Fuller, suggested more than forty years ago, we are entering a critical moment, a profound fork in the road. Utopia or Oblivion?

We have taken a first step into Utopia. Can it help us to move further down that path and avoid Oblivion?

# CHAPTER TWELVE

# BIOLOGY AND TECHNOLOGY MERGE

I n the Shift Age, biology and technology will merge to an unprecedented degree. Up until the twenty-first century, humans generally thought of these two areas as being separate. Biology concerned living things or matter. Technology related to man-made things and their uses. That was the clear way of thinking about these terms up until the later part of the twentieth century, when people began to think and begin to see the early possibilities of combining the two. Biology was of the earth, and technology was of humankind. Biology was about living things, and technology was about inanimate things created by man.

In the next decade, this integration of biology and technology will make us think anew about our long-held definitions of them. Centuries-old concepts of what life is and how it is created will be challenged.

We stand at the threshold of the redefinition of technology, biology, and ultimately life itself. Here are the current dictionary definitions of biology and technology.

**biology**

1. the science of life or living matter in all its forms and phenomena, especially with reference to origin, growth, reproduction, structure, and behavior.
2. the living organisms of a region: *the biology of Pennsylvania*.

3. the biological phenomena characteristic of an organism or a group of organisms: the biology of a worm.

—Dictionary.com

**technology**

1. the branch of knowledge that deals with the creation and use of technical means and their interrelation with life, society, and the environment, drawing upon such subjects as industrial arts, engineering, applied science, and pure science.

2. the terminology of an art, science, etc.; technical nomenclature.

3. a technological process, invention, method, or the like.

4. the sum of the ways in which social groups provide themselves with the material objects of their civilization.

—Dictionary.com

Toward the end of the twentieth century, the use of the word *technology* expanded to include and represent man-made processes that had been originally thought of merely as individual inventions. For example, in Gutenberg's time, his moveable-type press would have been called an invention, machine, or process. Today, it's considered a transformative technology. Once we entered the Information Age, the definition of technology changed to embrace many of man's inventions and their uses. *Technology* largely replaced the words *machine* or *machinery*.

Not so with biology. For instance, when the Human Genome Project was completed in 2003, it was about the deeper genetic underpinnings of humans. Even though the process to map it involved a lot of technology, it was not thought of as a technology, but rather a breakthrough in understanding the building blocks of humanity. So technology helped man to make a breakthrough with biology, but was still only considered a tool.

In the latter part of the twentieth century, humans began to combine man-made devices and biology. The heart pacemaker, the artificial heart valve, and the early generation of joint replacements commenced the bionic stage of medicine. In the last decade this has led to many other bio-technological innovations in medicine as well. Artificial limbs have been invented that ever more closely replicate the functions of natural limbs. Embedding smart chips in the body is now a developing reality. The field of neuroscience is in its glory time. We have learned more about how the brain functions in recent decades than in all of prior human history. In addition, nanotechnology will undergo explosive growth in the Shift Age. This is discussed in more detail in the Technology chapter, but overall nanotechnology will be bringing biology into technology and technology into biology at the molecular level. It is at this level that life and technology will have some interesting and transformative interactions and creations.

At the same time, breakthroughs in computing are happening at an accelerating pace. In 2010 a team of scientists led by Dr. Craig Venter successfully created synthetic life. Venter somewhat sensationally stated that it was the first life form created by computer.[1] This breakthrough will begin something that only existed in science fiction: man-made life! Artificial intelligence and human intelligence will to some degree always be separate, but it is clear that overlaps between the two will occur and that advances in each will spur the other. The progress down this path is something impossible to forecast. While science may well move quickly, the reality is that such progress will come up against all the thinking of humanity's history about what life is and God as the creator of life. Unfortunately, clashes of science and religion, with a large dose of politics, will likely have more influence more than scientific breakthroughs in shaping the possibilities over the next twenty years.

The only sure thing is that, in the Shift Age, actual discussion about creating synthetic life will occur for the first time.

# New Definitions in Biology and Technology

The Shift Age will see a fundamental change in the definitions of the words *biology* and *technology*. Though it may take years for the dictionary definitions shown previously to change, they are already beginning to change in the world today. Here are some of the developments ahead that will prompt redefinition:

> » Man-made technology will become part of biological man through bionics and implants
>
> » Man-made technology will be connected seamlessly to brains and neurological pathways in the body so that such things as bionic limbs will respond to directive thoughts from the brain
>
> » Genetics and stem cells will be used more frequently to create artificial organs in the laboratory
>
> » DNA and enzymes will be incorporated into computing, creating biological chips and computers
>
> » Artificial meat will be created in laboratory. Living, organic, healthy food, created in laboratories, will replace the live animals we consume that have been brutalized and drugged
>
> » Artificial insects and birds will perform functions in nature, such as pollination. These can be used for areas under ecological stress
>
> » Computers will be developed that are programmed to emote and that through time can develop true human emotions

This is just a partial list to convey some of the developments in the completely new and uncharted world that will be the result of merging man-made with nature-made. These efforts will make us reconsider what is from nature and what is from man. What is biological and what is technological. The development of much of this merging will occur during the Transformation Decade and will not reach the market or impact the daily lives of individuals until the 2020s.

The Shift Age will be the first age in human history when biology and technology merge in ways that will force us to rethink both words.

The merging of biology and technology will bring not just a change of definitions, but how we look at life and the definition of life itself.

# CHAPTER THIRTEEN

# AN EVOLUTIONARY SHIFT IN CONSCIOUSNESS

Years ago, when I was first formulating my thoughts about the Shift Age, one of the initial driving concepts was that humanity would, sometime in the not-too-distant future, experience an evolutionary shift in consciousness. Two years before my first book *The Shift Age* was published, I launched the blog www.EvolutionShift.com for this reason. When asked about the title, I simply stated that my belief in this impending change was why I chose the name. I had steeled myself for negative response. After all, it was a pretty radical thought. What surprised me, however, was the lack of ridicule I received. If this idea was not always accepted and embraced, it was at least something people considered.

There are several large contexts that most people have experienced that have opened them up to the possibility that this new evolutionary shift in consciousness might occur. These include the passage to a new century, a new age, and a new decade; the "dawning of the Age of Aquarius," an idea around since the 1960s, for those who follow astrology; and the increased awareness of the Mayan Prophecy of 2012, which predicts a transformative change for humanity on 12/21/12. All of these things have made people more receptive to at least the consideration that the age we are in may well usher in a new consciousness.

As I stated in the first chapter of this book, each age has been brought about by a significant development in a particular field that has spurred humanity's progress:

» Tools defined the Agricultural Age
» Machines defined the Industrial Age
» Technology defined the Information Age
» Consciousness will define the Shift Age

This expected shift in consciousness was one of the primary reasons that led me to give the Shift Age its name. Since approximately 2006, the year after the end of the Threshold Decades, almost everything in the world today is undergoing some rate of shift. Some of these shifts are evident in our daily lives, such as the Accelerated Electronic Connectedness of our world through the Internet and cellular connectivity, which has manifested in the devices we use to communicate and the different ways we do communicate. Some of these shifts are slower, such as the view of our stewardship of Spaceship Earth. The technological gadgets and innovations that come into our lives at an increasing rate alter our behavior immediately and make us aware of daily shifts that occur. Some other shifts are larger, or develop more slowly and thus are not immediately discerned. These will result in wide-scale change, but awareness of them spreads much more slowly through the population. Yet it is clear that massive and ongoing shift has happened, is happening, and will continue at varying rates of change. These shifts will affect all of humanity.

The Five Contexts of the Shift Age represent fundamental areas of change in perception and thinking. The first four (Earth Century, Retrofitting the Twentieth Century, the Changing Concept of Place, and the Merging of Biology and Technology) exemplify the necessity for a major adjustment in our thinking and letting go of legacy thought. They also reframe our concept of humanity. This fifth one, which I initially thought to be the hardest for others to comprehend and substantiate, is actually the one that, as a prediction, audiences around the world most readily agree to when I present it, if their nodding of heads and subsequent discussions are any indication. There is a clear growing sense of something approaching that is part consciousness and perhaps spirituality, part intuitive knowledge and growth. The recent wide circulation of such ideas as those mentioned at beginning of the chapter allows us to consider and perhaps anticipate that something new or different is approaching.

> What might this next evolutionary step of consciousness look and feel like, and what are the forces that are taking humanity toward it?

Let's start by addressing ideas and forces already discussed and looking at why they might be moving us toward this evolutionary shift.

# The Three Forces of the Shift Age
## THE FLOW TO GLOBAL

We are now in the global stage of human evolution. We have moved through all the earlier stages of human groupings that have influenced our consciousness: family, tribe village, city, city-state, and nation-state. Each one of these still exists, but they are now all subsets of the global whole. The first two, family and tribe, probably had the closest relationship to earth and nature, as that is where their awareness lay. For early humans, the rhythms of the earth shaped their entire consciousness. Once we moved to villages and cities, the Concept of Place began to take shape and with it the sense that humanity could in fact shape nature. City-states and nation-states developed the shared, collective consciousness of identity, heritage, manifest destiny, and, ultimately, nationalism. Certainly nationalism, race, and many of the major religions of the world have in the largest way created large-scale senses of separateness.

Now, with a sense of globalism entering into our daily lives in many ways, there is a growing appreciation by the larger populations of the world that we are all global citizens as well as citizens of cities and nations. Seers and visionaries such as Teilhard de Chardin and others may have seen this in years past, as the collective consciousness has been a vision held by many mystics and visionaries throughout the ages. But it's never been felt on such a grand scale as today. Every day, more and more of the 7-plus billion of us alive become aware of being connected to each other in ways that transcend the boundaries of state and religion. The reality of living in the Earth Century and feeling the finiteness of Spaceship Earth in our minds and in the way we live forces us toward a greater awareness of the interconnected whole that is humanity on earth, and therefore, toward a new consciousness.

## THE FLOW TO THE INDIVIDUAL

As discussed earlier, this flow has resulted in the Individual being ever more powerful. Today, we as individuals are more powerful than individuals have ever been before. We have increasingly been able to shape our identities around our own individuality, rather than subsuming it into larger organizations such as unions, country clubs, companies, etc. This releases an empowering sense of self-determination, self-definition, and self-identification, particularly when combined with the ever-faster connectivity that allows individuals to step beyond their place-based social and business groupings. This allows individuals to have a level of influence, sharing, and relationship with potentially anyone regardless of place. As individuals we put content out that can potentially reach millions of people. This opens up a shaping of the identity larger than ever before, allowing us to connect to each other as individuals regardless of where we live and what we belong to. As an individual, I can upload posts to my blog from anywhere in the world, and people from anywhere in the world can and do read the blog. As an individual, I am connecting with other individuals in a global, empowering way.

## ACCELERATING ELECTRONIC CONNECTEDNESS

This of course is one of the most powerful forces in the history of humanity. It eliminates time, distance, and place from communication. No longer must one be in a certain place to communicate with others there or in another place via a fixed wired connection. As explained in Chapter Eleven, the Concept of Place has changed forever, and with it a certain amount of the place-based consciousness that has defined humanity. In some way in all of us, more in some than others, this allows a historically unprecedented reality to not need to be defined by place.

Accelerating Electronic Connectedness has plugged most of us into each other. This screen reality, ever increasing in size, ever increasing in data, ever increasing in participation, ever increasing in importance, is lifting us up and away from our physical reality. This is creating the dual realities—screen reality and physical reality—discussed earlier. The visual image is of all our communications and searches becoming synapses of a cyberspace brain that pulses larger and more rapidly every day. This is the Neurosphere, which could be thought of as a technological space that is an early model or stage of the evolutionary shift in consciousness.

I have used the word *Neurosphere* in this book and for years in speeches and writings, even though there is no such word in the dictionary. We are all aware of the word *biosphere*, which is the Earth's surface and the atmosphere that supports life. Think of the word *Neurosphere* as a similar word that describes the pulsating, growing, technologically driven cyberspace that is the

**Neurosphere** can be viewed as a descendant or a derivative of Teilhard de Chardin's "noosphere." In his landmark books *The Phenomenon of Man* and *The Future of Man,* de Chardin suggested that evolution was a process that moves through increasing complexity toward what would ultimately be a unified consciousness. He used the word "noosphere" to describe the ever-increasing accumulation and expansion of the knowledge and interactions of humans: an ever-expanding sphere of human thought. He theorized that evolution must move toward ever more complexity and greater consciousness. He theorized that it might ultimately culminate in the Omega Point, some ultimate complex unification of consciousness.

The brilliance of de Chardin's thinking and depth of scholarship far surpasses my attempt to summarize it here. And he formulated his thoughts in the first half of the twentieth century without the obvious evidence I have of the Accelerating Electronic Connectedness of today. His brilliant vision seems eerily accurate when looking at where this third force of the Shift Age may well be taking us.

extension of all of our brain activity, and an ever-increasing amount of our knowledge, history, economic transactions, entertainment diversions, education, and, yes, identities.

In a similar manner, the Neurosphere should be viewed as a possible technological model or precedent for the shift in evolutionary consciousness that lies ahead. This becomes a more real consideration when looked at through the lens of the merging of biology and technology just discussed.

# Generations

In Chapter Fourteen, we look at the Shift Age generations. The Millennial Generation and the Digital Native Generation are clearly different from those that have preceded them. Of particular interest are the Digital Natives born since 1997, who have a completely different sense of themselves in this new connected world. How much different will a three-year-old who uses an iPad today be from a three-year-old in the middle part of the twentieth century whose only experience with a screen was a movie theater or television set? This first generation of the twenty-first century may well be the one to lead us into this next evolutionary shift of consciousness.

# Technology

We will be taking a quick look at technology in the Shift Age. One of the technologies that relates to a new developing consciousness is brainwave computer interface. This technology is in its infancy but will develop rapidly in the next few years. It will give us the ability to interact directly with computing devices using our brainwaves. Wearing a headset that maps our brainwaves, we will be able to think of functions and tasks and have a computing device perform them. Think about how we, particularly the Digital Natives, will quickly develop levels of concentration of laser-like precision.

This technology will also come to the gaming world, ultimately rendering the hand-held controller obsolete, or optional. Imagine competing with another gamer who also has a headset that maps their brainwaves into the game. If you lose your concentration, you will most likely lose.

From there, it's not too much of a leap from direct brain interaction with computers and advanced gaming devices to direct brainwave interaction with another human brain.

\* \* \*

## What Will This Next Evolutionary Shift of Consciousness Look Like?

Opening up to envisioning what it will be may be hard for many to do. Some people have a sense of what it might be, what it might feel like, and its inevitability. Others may have no way to understand what it might be or even to accept the reality of its happening. For those of you who are dismissive, please remember that there will be as much change in the next few decades as occurred in the last thousand years.

Think back to the year 2000 and imagine what your response would have been had I told you then that within ten years you would carry 1,000 CDs in your pocket, 100 books in your purse or briefcase; that you would have a few hundred friends connected to you sharing daily events and pictures; that you would carry one device in your pocket that handled email and contacts, took photos and videos, provided directions to where you wanted to go, and acted as a portal to answer any question you had about anything. Simply put, you would have asked if I was crazy or not feeling well. Now realize that all of these functions are the result of technology—smartphones, iPods, Kindles, and tablets—that you can hold in your hand.

In other words, the evolutionary consciousness shift that will define the Shift Age will be hard to accept as a probable reality from the vantage point of 2012. It will begin to come to us in a succession of technological innovations bringing our thoughts ever closer to each other. Bringing the ability to share experiential sensorial feelings with others, where we can actually sense their emotions.

First, new devices will come along in the next few years that will be smaller and more multifunctional than anything available today. We will have a continuing cascade of new gadgets that will empower us in ways we cannot yet fathom. For example, something like a small headset that will do whatever your voice says to do, no matter where you are. Call your son, change the thermostat, move documents, pictures, and videos to anywhere in the world.

Think of a device the size of your current app phone that is a holographic portal for a global meeting where you are all present in real time with realistic views of each other around a conference table. Global, holographic real-time collaboration taking a leap beyond video conferencing will not only further eliminate place and distance, it will create interactive dynamics that are 3D, not 2D. You may actually hug a loved one and feel it, regardless of where that loved one is.

> » Think of a headset that will cast your thoughts out into the Internet for a selected audience or to anyone.
> » Think of an emotionally sensitive touchscreen that will convey your emotional state to others.
> » Think of a small headset that, once individually programmed to your brainwaves, will allow you to communicate with your thoughts—to others connected to your frequency.

Sound like science fiction? Go back and read those predictions of 2000 that you would have also thought science fiction.

So we ascend to the technological level of brainwave and thought connectivity.

Second, there will be significant collective thought that will increasingly course through all communication channels as memes, thus developing a collective level of thought that takes the "memes to movements" concept to a more immediate and experiential level. The previously mentioned technology will increasingly connect our thoughts with others in a massive, rapid way. So we almost instantaneously connect with each other. Think of the speed of the Occupy movement. Think of the speed with which information courses through social media in 2012.

We will develop an ever more collective sense of each other as we live together as crew on Spaceship Earth. Our interconnectedness will be seen and felt as an increasing and developing reality on a physical, mental, and technological level.

Now we lift off and largely leave a lot of the above technology behind. Mind-to-mind communication. Unified consciousness. Direct, without technological intermediaries. We will take our ability to sense someone's emotional state today and combine it with this newly developed level of brain-to-brain interface. We will simply "know" what another person is thinking and certainly feeling.

Many of us have experienced that sensation of being connected to a loved one on a vibrational level when you can sense their emotional state from afar. Take that and multiply it by the thought vibrations of numerous others in close proximity and then expand out from there. Like Jedi knights who can feel the energy of the Force.

This collective consciousness will, for most of us, be something we will be able to access during conscious mindful practice, similar to meditation. Others, the vanguards and the more sensitive or attuned of us, will have unparalleled insight to massive amounts of thought, so much so that they will have to develop "blocks" to avoid neurological overload.

This unified field of consciousness will be one of incredible intensity, of incredible joy and beauty. A sense of union not yet experienced, on a wide scale, in human history. In a fully experienced form or state, it will transform humanity. It will also inevitably be accelerative, as it takes the age-old tensions between good and evil, positive and negative, to a higher, more intimate, and more influential level than ever before. That said, one of the underlying aspects of this evolutionary next step in human consciousness is that those who seek union, those who seek a higher consciousness, will most likely arrive at it first.

This is hard to imagine. Perhaps the way to do so is to recall those moments in your past when you felt love deeply, when the beauty of nature or music in church resonated to the core of your being, when you spoke the same thought at the same time as someone else. Then take these deeply personal moments and project them onto all of humanity.

Yes, a unified field of human consciousness will occur. In fact, the beginnings of this single consciousness are already in existence; we are simply too stuck in the tail end of our stage of evolutionary separateness to access it. But we will.

Welcome to the coming evolutionary shift in consciousness.

CHAPTER FOURTEEN

# THE SHIFT AGE GENERATIONS

The Shift Age is a time of great generational transfer of power, influence, and authority. It is perhaps the greatest generational transfer at the greatest speed in human history.

Looking at history and looking at the world through the lens of generations can, just as with any lens or filter, be limiting in its scope. Generalities prevail, values are assigned, and tens of millions of people are grouped together despite the full spectrum of individuality and uniqueness that we represent. That said, viewing the world through the lens of generations is helpful in assessing where we have been and where the changes in the world will trend. And there are two distinct generations that are and will be in ascendency in the Shift Age: the Millennials and the Digital Natives. Understanding these generations is crucial to succeeding in the Shift Age.

To recap our discussion in Chapter Eight, the Millennials are people who, as of 2012, are in their twenties and have come of age in this new millennium. There are two loose subsets of this group, as we will discuss shortly.

The Digital Natives are those young people who, as of 2012, are twenty and younger. The name "Digital Natives" is due to the reality that they are the first generation born into the new digital landscape.

As you can see, we're defining these generations in relation to their experience with the digital world. The Millennials were largely introduced as adolescents. Digital Natives entered the digital landscape as children. Everyone else is what I refer to as a "digital immigrant."

Anyone reading these words over the age of thirty in 2012 is unquestionably a digital immigrant. These adults have been introduced to the latest technology, devices, apps, and social media as adults. Digital immigrants largely comprise the Baby Boomers and Generation X.

Baby Boomers were born between 1946 and 1964. If you accept the approximate start of the Information Age to be in the mid-1970s, then the Baby Boomers were the first generation in history whose lifespan has been touched by three ages. They were born in the Industrial Age, spent most of their adult lives in the Information Age, and they have now entered the Shift Age. Prior to the Information Age, there never really was a generation that was not contained by a single age, which is why the Boomers are so unique.

That is why, for years, I have called them the Bridge Generation—they bridge, particularly in the developed countries of the world, the end of the Industrial Age into the beginning of the Shift Age. In all areas of society, they are the bridge to the second half of the twentieth century. They also therefore hold the greatest amount of legacy thinking, which, as discussed in Chapter Seven, is now falling away at an almost incomprehensible rate.

Of course, the problem with Boomers having so much legacy thought is that it has always been about them. They have been the pig in the python in terms of shaping social thought. That is why, as you must have experienced if you are a Boomer or a Millennial, the workplace has become a battleground between these two generations. Boomers think about how they "came up" or became successful and don't realize how different the Millennials are. The Millennials, in addition to feeling misunderstood, hold resentment for the conditions created by the Boomers. For example, the Millennials had nothing to do with the global reorganizational recession of 2007–2012. It was largely a Baby Boomer collapse. A college graduate with a fresh diploma from the classes of 2008–2010 graduates into the worst economic mess in seventy-five years and sees it as the doing of the Baby Boom Generation.

Generation X is sandwiched between the Boomers and the Millennials. In the workplace, they spend much of their time translating the Millennials to the Boomers and trying to get the Millennials to not completely dismiss all Boomer thinking as out of date.

Gen X is the generation the spotlight missed. One of the Gen X experiences, however, is that, in 2012 and for the next decade, they will be the largest group of parents of K–12 students, all of whom are Digital Natives. This gives Gen X a personal insight into this incredible new developing consciousness and rewiring of the brain that the Digital Natives represent.

# The Millennial Generation

Volumes have been written and numerous research studies have been done about the Millennial Generation, and various timeframes have been given for their earliest and latest birth years. Once more, it must be said that specifically defining any generation must be done with some license of categorization that is not neat and specific but general, indicative, and directional. Things bleed both ways before and after arbitrary dates, but writing and speaking about generations is always somewhat arbitrary. With that said, I see the Millennial Generation as those largely born between 1981 and 1997 (that means that as of this writing, in 2012, they are 15 to 31 years old), those who grew up with the digital world but were not born into it.

For me the single greatest demarcation of how this generation is defined and segmented is technological. Those members of this generation born in the 1980s first experienced the Internet as teenagers. Their first experience with the Internet was dial-up or early-stage broadband but all connected with wires and cords; wireless was a second-stage experience of connectivity for them. Through this technological lens, the Millennial Generation can be segmented into two groups, those born between 1981 and 1991 and those born between 1991 and 1997.

The older group moved through the early stages of Internet connectivity into what it is today. The younger group stepped into connectivity when it was high speed and wireless. The older group had significant experience with early-generation cell phones, without Internet connectivity, before moving to smartphones and then app phones. The younger group often had a smartphone or an app phone as their first phone.

In his book *Hooked Up*, published in July 2012, Jack Myers coined the phrase "Internet Pioneers" to describe Millennials born between 1991 and 1995. Myers makes the distinction that the Millennials born during this five-year period are really the first generation to fully grow up with the Internet and are therefore profoundly different from those born before. His research supports this view, one I completely agree with. The only difference I have from Myers's grouping of Internet Pioneers is that I would extend their birth years to 1997. This is because all of Myers's research was done on Americans. I take a more global view, so adding the additional two years takes into consideration that other developed countries lag behind America, the Internet leader of the world.

So now that we have defined who the Millennials are, let's take a close look at how they view the world and how they will shape the coming years. Since a number of books have already been written about the Millennial Generation and their qualities, I will only focus here on the reality that they are the first of two generations to come of age and move into society in the Shift Age.

The Milllenials will be the first new adult generation of the Shift Age. As they move into their ever-more-connected place in society, the workplace, and culture around the world, they will dramatically accelerate the collapse of legacy thinking. They will initiate magnitudes of change in all areas of life. Their thinking, behavior, morals, and worldview will be the ascendant ones of the Shift Age. They will reach pinnacles of organizational power in the 2020s, when the first of their generation will become leaders of national politics, multinational organizations, and cultural and nonprofit organizations.

The Milllenials came into adulthood under the specter of the September 11, 2001 attacks in America. This means that for most, if not all, of their lives they have seen only war, as the wars of Iraq and Afghanistan have been going on for a significant part of their lives. Though to many of this generation these wars are indeed remote, tens of thousands of older Millennials from around the world have served in these two wars.

I had an interesting personal experience in my role as Futurist in Residence and Guest Lecturer at the Ringling College of Art + Design, where some of the most talented and gifted creative Millennials from around the world are students. In the fall of 2011, I was speaking to a class about the dynamics of the Shift Age. After of course asking them to close their laptops and take their hands off their phones, I asked them this question:

"Why, as a Baby Boomer, did I have an emotional reaction when I woke up this morning and saw that the date was November 22?"

Not one of them knew the answer. I was startled.

"November 22, 1963 was the day President John F. Kennedy was assassinated," I said, feeling emotion still.

I challenged them on their lack of knowledge, at which point a student said:

"That may be an important date for your generation, but our date is 9/11."

Now think about that interchange within the contexts of the Baby Boom Generation's being the Bridge Generation and legacy thinking.

This led to a discussion of their reality that, ever since they were children, America has always been at war. Since this was a communications class, and one aspect of the class was to create a class communications project, I led a brainstorming session about what that project might be.

"Well, how about a project about peace?" I suggested.

Shortly thereafter a female student raised her hand and said: "But we don't know what peace looks like."

We then quickly came up with a project, which was to ask the question of their generation and, more importantly, their parents' generation: "What does peace look like?"

The hope was to create a meme in which Millennials around the world stood up and asked their elders, "What does peace look like?" "Why have we never seen peace?"

The poignancy of this interchange and question is both clear and powerful. The Millennials are coming of age and moving into and up in all areas of human endeavor with a clearly different and somewhat unencumbered view of the twenty-first century and the Shift Age, an age they will largely shape.

This generation has grown up having less gender and racial bias. They have grown up with a much more global sense of themselves, they are much more collaborative and collective in their thinking, and they are coming into adulthood at a time of great economic hardship. When they see and experience the incredibly high levels of unemployment for their generation around the world, they realize that they didn't have anything to do with it. This leads them to often disregard the suggestions, ideas, directions, and points of view of older generations. This creates a huge generational gap of worldview between the Millennials and their elders.

This gap will accelerate the collapse of legacy thinking in the Transformation Decade, as the Millennial Generation will not respect, embrace, or buy into the legacy thinking of the Bridge Generation and Generation X.

So legacy thinking will not be passed along generationally to the degree that it has been in the past. That is why Millennials will be the ones to come up with the innovative and transformative ideas needed to retrofit the twentieth century. They will be the ones that show the way to solving the global problems of the twenty-first century.

The catastrophic reorganizational global recession between the Information Age and the Shift Age from 2007 to 2012, with incredibly high unemployment percentages in the Millennial Generation, has also changed the economic aspirations of this generation. Since the traditional paths to employment have closed, since the college degree they are now in debt to pay off is not being honored in the traditional job space, they are increasingly viewing entrepreneurship as their future. We are going to see a higher percentage of entrepreneurship and levels of independent contractors in this generation starting at an earlier age than ever before.

# Digital Natives

As interesting and powerfully influential as the Millennial Generation is, I am equally if not more fascinated by the Digital Natives. As a futurist, it is this generation I have been observing closely, as they provide a view on what will be a brand-new level of awareness and consciousness in the Shift Age.

> To recap the discussion in Chapter Seven, Digital Natives are defined by the ever-more-rapid technological change of the last fifteen years. As with the Millennials before them, I divide this generation into two groups. The first wave of Digital Natives was born between 1997 and 2009; the second has been born since 2010.

The first wave of this generation has never experienced a time without the Internet, mobile phones, or high-speed wireless connectivity. They have grown up with Search as a reality and immediate option. As children, they had all of the world's knowledge just a few keystrokes away. They are the first generation born into the earlier-described reality of no-placeness, of being able to communicate with and connect to anyone and anyplace in the world.

Another way of thinking about the Digital Natives is through the lens of what most Boomers and Gen Xers call "information overload." I think that one of the most often-asked questions I have gotten from audiences all around the world is something along the lines of "How can I keep up, how can I deal with information overload?" This, of course, is quite understandable to you members of either of those two generations. The Digital Natives, though, are the first generation born into the connected, information-overloaded world. Since this is all they have ever known, they don't think of it as overload, just reality.

As parents, we have all seen this with our teenaged and younger children. They sit with the television on, connected to the Internet, maintaining multiple text conversations, while listening to music on their earbuds. No stress, just hyperprocessing of incoming and available data.

All of the technological inventions and innovations of the Information Age—computers, fax machines, communication satellites, cable television, mobile phones, Internet, laptops, tablets, high-speed wireless connectivity, Search, social media—are things that all previous generations, including the Millennials born in the 1980s, came to through time. The Digital Natives are the first generation for whom all these things were available to them as children. Every prior generation has had to adapt to these inventions and, to some degree, alter established behavior to do so after childhood. To the Digital Natives, this is their reality.

> Digital Natives are the first generation of the twenty-first century. There is no remembrance, legacy thinking, established pattern of behavior, thought, or cultural context from the twentieth century. They are a clean-slate generation.

If you will accept my earlier premise from Chapter Two that the Shift Age started around 2006, then the oldest Digital Native was nine and just entering the fourth grade. So this is the first completely new generation of the Shift Age.

Now, why do I divide the Digital Natives based upon birth years 1997–2009 and 2010 and after? Think about what transpired with connectivity and technology during the years 2010–2012:

> » Global cell phone connectivity crossed 70 percent
> » Touchscreens became the norm
> » The iPad was introduced, starting the computing migration to tablets
> » App phones—iPhones and Android phones—achieved market dominance in the smartphone market segment in the United States
> » 3G, then 4G, high-speed wireless connectivity became commonplace in many countries
> » Ebook readers took off in the United States and ebooks as a percentage of books sold dramatically increased
> » DVDs gave way to streaming
> » Smart music platforms such as Pandora and Spotify grew dramatically

So, a two-year-old in 2012, in a middle-class or above household, has screens everywhere, many of them touchscreens. From the app phone to the tablet, to the laptop to the flat-screen television, screens were and are ubiquitous. Digital Natives' first awareness of and consumption of content was all on screens.

This second wave of Digital Natives will never remember content that was not available on a screen. This second wave will never remember not having touchscreens. This second wave will never remember a time when they couldn't interact via video with anyone anywhere in the world, live. Everything from anywhere and at any time is available on a screen. This means that this second wave of Digital Natives will be the first generation for whom the screen reality may well be the dominant reality they experience. They will be the first generation that knows no lack or limitation because of place.

This points to the special reason I am fascinated by the Digital Natives and particularly the ones born since 2010. They simply will have a different consciousness than any preceding generation. As they grow up, this will become increasingly clear.

In the last chapter I touched on the probable evolutionary shift in human consciousness that will be a defining part of the Shift Age. I have always thought that this might start to occur in the 2020s. When will the oldest Digital Native turn twenty-one? 2018. When will the first of the second wave of this generation turn twenty-one? 2030. (To bring this down to the old traditions of the physical reality, the United States will have a Digital Native as President in the 2040s, following the first or second Millennial President.)

So this coming of age of the Digital Native generation will be one of the strongest influences on this evolutionary step of human consciousness. Of course, there will be people from preceding generations that will make this shift as well, but they will have had to let go of something from the past to do so.

In my speeches around the world, I regularly speak about the Digital Native generation. I have noticed a clear distinction in audiences around the world during question-and-answer sessions after my speeches. People who do not have children or grandchildren under the age of fifteen ask the questions around the issues of whether the young are losing the ability to concentrate and whether they are becoming superficial and distracted in their thinking. This, of course, comes from the conversation in the zeitgeist that has been going on since the Internet became central to our lives. The "Are we raising a generation of distracted and superficial children?" type of thinking.

Usually a parent of a child fifteen or younger will then raise their hand to comment on some remarkable thing their child learned, did, connected to, or created that was way beyond anything they could even imagine doing at the same age. Even more delightfully is the white-haired grandparent who will talk about how their three- or four-year-old grandchild matriculated through all levels of a game on an iPad that they themselves could not master. Here is a short list of anecdotes I have heard from people:

» A four-year-old who can count to twenty, knows addition, and is learning multiplication with an iPad

» A three-year-old who has cracked the password to download a bunch of paid apps on his grandfather's iPhone, in fifteen minutes

» A seven-year-old who taught himself PowerPoint on his father's iPad and asked if he could take it to school to deliver his homework that way

» An eighteen-month-old who can successfully search YouTube to find his favorite animated characters.

» A three-year-old who opened up Skype and called his grandmother while his parents were out because he wanted to ask his grandma a question

» Three ten-year-olds who used Google Docs to collaborate on a fourth-grade class project

Again, we must think about how differently these children are growing up and how intuitively they interact with, utilize, and manipulate technology and connectivity as they do so.

The Digital Natives

» have no memory of the twentieth century

» have only known Accelerating Electronic Connectedness

» expect to be able to connect to cyberspace, a spatial place no prior generation has ever experienced from birth, so space means as much as place to them

» will accept technology, not technique, as the means for creating art in all forms

» may well be the first generation to grow up thinking of themselves as global citizens first and foremost

» will, as a generation, have greater synaptic activity in their brains at any age than any prior generation

» will have a significant percentage of their generation live into the twenty-second century

The Digital Natives, the first generation fully of the Shift Age, will grow up in ways no generation ever has. They will be the generation that will guide us and help us into the evolutionary next step of consciousness.

In summary, the Millennial Generation and the Digital Native Generation will be the two dominant generations of the Shift Age. The Millennial Generation will be the leaders across the board as we exit the Transformation Decade. The Digital Natives will lead us into new realms of creativity and consciousness never before experienced.

# CHAPTER FIFTEEN

# THE ASCENDENCY
# OF WOMEN

In the previous chapter, we explored how the Shift Age will be a time of transfer of generational power. Now we will look at how it will also be a time of ascendency for women. There will be a greater alteration in the view of gender and in the equalization of women with men than in any prior age. When the Shift Age gives way to the next age one of the clear historical realities will be how the entire view of gender will have undergone unprecedented change.

This of course is due in part to the great flow toward equality for women that occurred in the Information Age. In the 10,000 years of the Agricultural Age and 300 years of the Industrial Age, there was a need for physical strength in much of the workplace. Working the fields with tools, forging iron, or constructing buildings without machines required strength. Then, when machines were invented, they required strength to operate. It has been generally accepted by historians and economists that, in the Agricultural and Industrial Age, physical strength was much more a necessary requirement for work than in the Information Age. Men's bodies were generally stronger and more suited to strenuous labor. This meant the development of the dual roles of the man who went out into the world to work and the woman who did the work of the home. Similarly, in war, men were the ones in combat, while women tended to play a sideline role or were kept removed from the action.

Inequalities abounded from this separation of the sexes. It is worth remembering that in the United States, the Declaration of Independence, creating what is now the oldest continuous democracy in the world, was signed over 236 years ago, and for 144 of those years it was illegal for women to vote. The language "all men are created equal" meant just that for the founders of the country. So, not only were woman largely excluded from widespread participation in the economy, they were legally excluded from participating as citizens in the electing of government officials.

Then, when the Information Age began in the mid-1970s, things began to rapidly change. In an information- and knowledge-based economy, strength was no longer a prerequisite for many jobs. This meant that performance on the job moved away from the major difference of the sexes, physical strength. Mental acuity, performance, efficiency, intelligence, collaboration, and all the skills needed in this new knowledge-based economy could no longer be delineated by male or female. Women had been voting for fifty years in the United States, so they had been, politically speaking, equal citizens, which further highlighted the clear inequality in the workplace. Women, metaphorically represented by Rosie the Riveter, had shown their capability to work the Industrial Age production lines during World War II. Old sexist stereotypes were now openly and successfully challenged in almost every industry across the board. For the first time, many skilled women, if they were allowed to, could successfully do the work and compete with men at the same skill level.

The women's liberation movement in the developed countries of the world was also in full force at the inception of the Information Age. Women rightfully demanded equality and fought their way into all forms of institutions that had either excluded them or had greatly limited their participation: corporations, private clubs, the military, universities, and the sciences. Most famously, Title IX became law in the United States in 1972, creating equality in all levels of education, most famously in athletics. By the 1980s, when it was clear that we were in the Information Age, the landscape of gender equality had changed, and fundamental change moved throughout the developed countries of the world.

So, think of a fifty-year arc from 1975 to 2025, from the beginning of the Information Age to the zenith of the Shift Age. View this arc as the trajectory of women in all aspects of society. As this book is being written in 2012, we are 75 percent of the way through this fifty-year passage. Think of all the change that has occurred in this time. An incredible amount when looked at through the longer lens of civilization as suggested in this fifty-year arc. However, this change will be easily met and surpassed by the remaining 25 percent to 2025. The amount of change, the amount of flow to women, the amount of power that women will gain in almost every area of human endeavor in the next thirteen years will match and almost assuredly exceed the last thirty-seven years.

## WHY THE RISE FOR WOMEN?

There are many directional signs clearly in view to point to this ascendency of women. In higher education, women are now in dominance. An important thing to note is that the Shift Age generations have much less of the sexism of preceding generations. Partly this is due to the rapid development of our screen reality, which lessens any need for physical strength. The old management models of hierarchies are also giving way to more net-like structures, which play more to women. These signs point to accelerating ascendancy of women between 2012 and 2025.

# Current Realities

Today there is still a huge disparity between the number of women in the population and the number of women in top positions of corporate and political power. This is primarily due to the legacy thinking of generations preceding the Millennials that still holds sway in modern society. These are the generations that were born largely before the Information Age and are still dominant in power positions such as top levels of government, large public corporations, the military, and higher education.

What must be looked at are the trends and the directions of those trends. When looking at the direction of this fifty-year arc, it is clear that it points toward equality at the very least, and perhaps even superiority in the 2020s.

The number of women in top management in corporations has been consistently increasing in the last ten years.[1] The number of political leaders that are women has been increasing during this time as well. This will continue in the developed countries of the world. In the developing countries it is occurring as well (the female-majority Parliament in Rwanda is a good example of this), but they lag slightly behind developed countries, as their move toward gender equality began a bit later.

Perhaps the single most significant fact that portends the future of greater female empowerment is that in many developed countries the ratio of women to men in the realm of higher education has dramatically changed from the Information Age. In the United States and most European countries, close to 60 percent of undergraduates were women in 2012.[2] In the area of advanced degrees, women are now in the majority at the master's level and in many doctorate programs. So in the entire area of higher education, women now numerically dominate.[3] This is a historical first. Decades of research show that the higher the degree, the greater the potential in terms of employment and earnings. There is no reason to think that this reality will change. Project this trend into the next twenty years and the conclusion is clear: women are stepping into this new reality in far greater numbers than men.

> It must be noted that the simple acquisition of a baccalaureate, master's, or PhD degree is no guarantee of fully actualized employment. The reorganizational global recession of 2007–2012 clearly has shown that degrees in and of themselves are no guarantee of employment. This leads to the reevaluation and transformation that will occur in higher education during the Shift Age. However, during the Shift Age, women are partaking and will partake of higher education in greater numbers than men in the developed countries of the world. Again, this is a direction. Ascendency is occurring through time.

There have been many analyses and studies done to answer the sociological question as to why this has happened. That interests me less than the fact that it is. If there is a general reason, it may well be simply that the thrust of women's equality that was launched at the beginning of the Information Age is so strong that it trumps the long-held cultural acceptance men have always had. For women, college is a stronger necessity in society today.

# Generations

In the last chapter we looked at the Millennial and Digital Native Generations, the Shift Age generations. Now let's look at how these generations will play a critical role in this ascendency of women.

The Millennial Generation, particularly those born after 1991, are noticeably less tied to the traditional ideas of gender roles in society than their parents. Partially, this is because this generation has a much more tribal and collective approach to all that they do. The Boomers grew up going out on dates or double dates. Growing up, the Millennials asked their parents to drive a "group of us" to the mall. Hundreds of Boomer and Gen-X parents in audiences around the world have spoken to me of this generational difference in dating. Millenials grew up socializing in groups, not pairs. They grew up in a world where women were expected to have equality with men, an expectation and reality that is relatively commonly accepted by both genders.

The Millennial Generation will move into the workplace and all other areas of society with many fewer of the gender stereotypes held by those before them. Those before them had to adapt to the new gender realities. This leadership generation of the Shift Age is much more of a clean slate in that regard. There will not be the issues around what male and female roles are to the degree that existed in the Boomer and Gen-X generations.

The Digital Natives will be even freer of any legacy thinking of gender roles. Equality, a global view, connectivity, and the screen reality guide this generation from their earliest experiences. As adults, they will learn about the history of gender inequality and the mistreatment of women through the twentieth century and be stunned how unfair and barbaric it was.

The Millennials and Digital Natives will test the subservient status of women in religions, particularly the ultra-conservative or conservative arms, like none before them. Not only is it not of their generations to understand it, it is of their generations to be globally connected. Girls raised in such religions where women are not equal have historically accepted such inequality, as that is how they were brought up. Now, with global connectivity, they will see that other girls their age are treated equally.

One of the truly great qualities of the Accelerated Electronic Connectedness force is that it can and will obliterate ignorance. Sects and cults, and to some degree the extremely conservative parts of traditional religions, have always used isolation or separation for thought control, keeping information out except what the leaders want their followers to be exposed to.[4] Now that humanity is universally connected, such control will be challenged and tested by these Shift Age generations.

## Screen Reality

As first discussed in Chapter Five, we now live in two realities, physical reality and screen reality. We live in a broadband world, so we have the physical reality of where we are and the screen reality we can access wherever we are. Prior to the Accelerated Electronic Connectedness of humanity, there was only physical reality to manage. Screen reality, as discussed in other chapters, is morphing much more rapidly than physical reality and is in fact is dramatically altering physical reality.

> Screen reality is gender neutral. Fewer physical inequalities or gender distinctions will exist on screen reality. As the world moves into screen reality, the historical gender distinctions based in a physical reality will become ever more antiquated.

Screen reality is moving us toward the new consciousness of the Shift Age. The screen reality is also the one that the Shift Age generations grew and are growing up with, so this amplifies even more the equalizing effect of screen reality for all of humanity, let alone women. The ever greater emphasis on the screen reality we have all experienced in recent years deemphasizes the physical reality that men have historically dominated.

# Structures and Hierarchies to Nets and Nodes

As discussed in Chapter Two, we as a society are moving from having physical structures as metaphors and dominant images to having networks as dominant metaphors and images.

The Industrial Age triggered centralization and urbanization. Early commercial enterprises had to create management to run these new centralized entities, and the only model was the military with its hierarchical chain of command model. This began the era of modern management that certainly thrived through this age. Hierarchical management was the dominant model. It was one created entirely by men, for men. We will never know how different hierarchies might have been had women created them. We therefore have to look at hierarchies as a male creation.

The Information Age was the transition between the hierarchical, structured model of the Industrial Age and the flat, networked model of the Shift Age. Companies eviscerated middle management; flattening the corporation became all the rage and the reality. Information technology allowed this to happen. Still, hierarchies ruled, and companies had silos and divisions that were both complimentary and competitive. Information moved across these silos, and top-down communication remained.

The Shift Age is about networks, flat management structures, and a high degree of collaboration. The model is the net, not the high rise; the net, not the hierarchy. This will further serve women as they move past equality to supremacy. Nets promote collaboration and social interaction. Women tend to be more collaborative and social than men.[5] Physical power is irrelevant. Authority is much less relevant than in hierarchies. Men, perhaps due to centuries of experience, are more hierarchical than women. Now hierarchies are viewed as outdated and slow to act or move.

I have advised many CEOs that though they cannot immediately move away from management structures, they must start to think of management as moving toward the model of a net. Nets have nodes. Corporate nodes might be finance, sales, and marketing. Management will now be thought of as nodal. This will result in huge changes in how companies operate. Connected networks move information much faster than hierarchies, so companies can and will make faster decisions and move more quickly in the marketplace. This move to networks and nodal management will empower women, as social connectedness will trump hierarchical authority. In Chapter Twenty-Five we look at how power will move from Control Power (read: hierarchical power) to Influence Power (read: networked power). All of this fundamental change in how organizations operate and how power is changing will amplify this ascendant arc for women in the Shift Age.

## Summary

There are many dynamics of the Shift Age that clearly point to its being the first age in which women will be truly ascendant. While actual physical strength and power may be an advantage men continue to have over women, the old social, cultural, and economic power that has traditionally defaulted to men will rapidly fall away. That said, men need not worry that they will be eclipsed or lose relevance in this shift.

The ascendancy of women in the Shift Age is not a battle of the sexes won by women and should not be looked at that way. Rather, it is a very significant evolutionary step in the humanity-long history of both sexes. Most if not all of the social, physical, and cultural forces that have defined men and women since the beginning of the Agricultural Age are in dramatic shift. Future historians will look back at the Information Age as the seeding and the beginning of these shifts that are happening and will happen in the Shift Age. The Shift Age will be viewed by these future historians, male and female, as the first age of humanity when women finally and fully shared in the shaping of history.

I sense that some of this massive shift will result in the redefining of gender as it relates to human society. The Shift Age will usher in a reconsideration or an extreme lessening of gender differences and social roles. Perhaps the only definition that will be in place is the gender distinction of childbirth. This in fact could actually accentuate and amplify the ascendency of women in a world where many of the global issues we now face flow from the significant population explosion of the last seventy-five years.

The stewardship of Spaceship Earth will in part be shaped by how humanity chooses what level of global population to embrace and sustain. What if, in the Earth Century, collective global humanity decided that fewer people would create greater happiness and sustainability far into the future? This could be done by simply deciding to procreate once. Without killing or sterilization, the population could be dramatically reduced by every woman deciding to only procreate once. Women would control this process much more than men. Women would lead the way in any path toward global sustainable population levels, if that becomes the significant issue I suspect it will be in several decades.

At this higher level, when it is looked at through the filter of Ages, I think that the Shift Age will be viewed as the transitional time from the reality of millennia of assumed male dominance to the reality of assumed gender equality and very probably female dominance.

## CHAPTER SIXTEEN

# TECHNOLOGY

The technological future of the Shift Age could easily be an entire book. In fact, there could be entire books on many of the individual technological transformations, inventions, and iterations briefly discussed in this chapter. But I am a futurist, not a technologist, so this chapter will address, at a high and simple level, the areas and types of technology that will come into being during this age and, equally importantly, how these technologies might alter the lives of many of us if not all of us.

In this chapter, I have grouped these technologies into two segments.

» The first are the technologies that are now coming into market-place acceptance and are therefore in early-stage influence.
» The second are those technologies that could be and will be invented and come to market in the next ten to twenty years.

These two groups are respectively called Emerging Transformative Technologies and Transformative Technologies of the Future.

It is clear to me from questions I have frequently been asked after talks and speeches that many people equate the future with technology, that those two things are one and the same or at least very close to it. To most people, the future becomes apparent through the new technological devices and services that come into their lives. Cell phones, laptops, tablets, app phones, etc., tumble into our lives. We both become dependent on them and establish intimate relationships with them. So that is what most people experience as the future, as it is these new devices that immediately change our behavior and provide a glimpse into the newness ahead. We learn to use GPS and map apps for driving, news apps to bring us the latest news, restaurant and movie apps to get reviews and buy tickets or make reservations, and all of this from wherever we may be. The tech gadgets that connect us are the "bright, shiny objects" of the Shift Age.

What people miss is that it is not the technology and the features—3G, 4G, this much RAM, that many gigahertz—it is the power that the technology gives to us, to our customers, to our competitors that is important. I have called this "power to the people." For example, a CEO of a global corporation can, with good bandwidth and one or two app phones or a tablet, run her company for a day from a park bench. That is the power behind the device.

> The key thing to focus on, whenever there is some breakthrough device, is just that: what power it gives to the user and what effect this new power may have on existing structures, business models, modes of communication, or information dissemination—all of which deeply affect every aspect of our lives.

# Emerging Transformative Technologies
## THE CLOUD

Cloud computing has left its infancy and is firmly in rapid growth mode. All aspects of our digital lives are now in or moving to "the Cloud." Very simply, this is the migration of data from one's own or one's company's servers and storage facilities to a remote server or servers. Through the use of shared storage facilities, companies and individuals can have ready access to vast amounts of data, software, programs, photos, videos, and all forms of digital files. Storage costs drop, backing up data becomes automatic, and access can be from anywhere. To recap the definition from Chapter Five, cloud computing allows people to instantly access vast amounts of data via portable devices. The Cloud is always available to us, wherever we might be.

Cloud computing is also an accelerant to global collaboration, as people from multiple time zones can collaborate in real time to work on the same document or project. This of course further accelerates the speed of business, the immediacy of interaction, and the evisceration of place.

Since the Cloud and cyberspace in general will be the space where there will be future conflicts and crime, it will always be good to have a secure physical backup of one's most critically important digital files. There will be incidences in the future of wide-scale attacks on the Cloud, and even though security in the Cloud is in most cases superior to standard firewalls, there will be incidences of systems and services being taken down from time to time.

Cloud computing will be ubiquitous by 2015. It is in fact a core ingredient of some of the other technological trends that follow.

## MOBILE COMPUTING

The hand-held device is the screen of the future. Cloud computing will allow us to access our data from anywhere. Computing is therefore moving to the mobile platform. 2012 is the first year in the United States when mobile computing devices will outsell PCs and other non-mobile computing devices.[1] Ever faster wireless connectivity will enable us to all communicate via video with anyone in the world. The office is wherever you are. The movie theater is wherever you are. All of the world's knowledge will always be available wherever you are.

> As it grows, this now-present reality will amplify and accelerate all areas of society and further diminish the Concept of Place. If you can access everything from wherever you are, it doesn't matter where you are.

The lifeline of society, of every nation going forward, will be robust, ever faster wireless connectivity. A productive society now means a connected society. Lower-cost wireless connectivity means ever more equality. An urban dweller in the United States can basically access the world for the price of a cup of coffee. The breadth and speed and cost of high-speed wireless connectivity will increasingly be a measurement of the vibrancy and potential of any country. It will also be an essential building block for any economy. It will be a very clear indicator of how countries feel about freedom and equality.

Mobile computing goes a long way towards addressing the issues of the Earth Century and Spaceship Earth. In Chapter Nine I wrote about the Earth Century as being one of the five contexts of the Shift Age. It is in this, the twenty-first century, that humanity has become the single greatest influence on the biosphere. Humanity will look at the twenty-first century as the time when stewardship of the Earth is part of our responsibility. With mobile computing, people can be productive without having to drive multi-ton vehicles that consume fossil fuels. We can work with less. We can do more with less. We can learn and share anything from anywhere.

## CONSUMERIZATION OF TECHNOLOGY

From the Industrial Age to well into the Information Age, technology usually showed up first at government or business workplaces, as they were the only type of institutions that could afford the high costs of new and powerful technologies. For instance, the mainframe computer, because of its tremendous costs and the skilled manpower needed to maintain it, could only be found in these environments. These mainframes had entire air-conditioned rooms staffed by the new hierarchical clergy of the computer age: Systems Analysts, Programmers, and Computer Operators.

These anointed humans, often dressed in white lab coats, were the interface for the rest of us with this new godlike technology: the computer.

Even in the Information Age, the beginning of the age of the PC, this usage pattern continued, though computing became much more widespread. But early fax machines and powerful printers were only in offices. Finally, in the 1990s, laptops made significant market penetration and PCs dropped significantly in cost, which greatly expanded the number of users. Even still, these users were primarily in business.

Moore's Law kept kicking in, lowering the cost and increasing the power of computing.[2] The cost of storage plummeted, the power of chips increased, the size of all things became ever smaller. Then, as we entered the Shift Age, the equation flipped and the commodification of technology began. Chief Technology Officers everywhere had to suddenly cope with the reality that the employees of their company and even the C-level executives were doing all kinds of cool, efficiency-increasing things with app phones and wondered why they couldn't have them integrated into the company's enterprise technology. In other words, CTOs, the lords of the tech manor in major institutions, were having to play catch-up to all the cool functionality individuals were carrying around with them on inexpensive devices. Again, "power to the people" leading the way.

I now sit in a hotel room with more computing power, speed, and storage than NASA had in the 1960s.[3] How remarkable! That is power to the people.

However, it goes beyond just the power and computing capability of our personal devices. These devices have allowed us to become ever more powerful and connected as consumers. Our hand-held devices let us continue increasing our shared power as consumers who have knowledge at our fingertips, wherever we are, to make faster decisions on just about everything. A group of people can quickly become a flash mob through their hand-held connectivity, something unimaginable ten or fifteen years ago. The Flow to the Individual merges with Accelerating Electronic Connectedness to drive power, choice, technological wizardry, and social connectivity to the consumer.

## AUGMENTED REALITY

In the next ten years, Augmented Reality will become a game changer in many areas of our lives. It is a new level of reality. If you are unfamiliar with the concept of "augmented reality," here is the current dictionary definition:

> an enhanced version of reality created by the use of technology to overlay digital information on an image of something being viewed through a device (as a smartphone camera); also: the technology used to create augmented reality
>
> —Merriam-Webster Online Dictionary

This is like defining a computer in the 1960s as a high-speed computation machine; it provides no insight into the unfathomable potential that inherently exists in this new technology.

In 2012, augmented reality is just beginning to enter our lives, but in ways that point to what it can become. Early manifestations are:

» apps on phones that allow you to point the camera at a bus stop and see the entire routes of the buses that stop there

» apps on phones that allow you to point your phone at a restaurant and read reviews posted online

» apps on phones that provide detailed information about the building, museum, or landmark as you look at it through your phone

» glasses that you wear that provide data about what you are looking at. The reality in front of you is enhanced with live, streaming data about whatever it is that you are looking at.

In other words, augmented reality is taking what we see in physical reality and adding in all the known information from the screen reality to it. In essence, it is a merging of these two realities in real time wherever we are.

The first level of both transformation and market acceptance will be when vast numbers of people start wearing augmented reality glasses or carrying smartphones with augmented reality apps. Whatever a person sees will be augmented beyond what is actually in the physical reality. Curiosity will be immediately satisfied. In fact, at some point, the answers to questions will be provided faster than the person can think of the question. We will all move through time and space with an enhanced experience that will be truly transformative and mind-altering.

This first phase of augmented reality will obviously lead to new business models and applications. Apps will be provided free by marketers wanting to keep brand awareness literally in front of the consumer. Deeper levels of augmentation beyond the basic levels may cost additional amounts of money, most likely on a subscription basis. Special versions of augmented reality apps could be sold. For example, architects and people in the construction business could look at buildings and see the schematics and all the utilities. This could help in any rehab or retrofitting work in addition to immediate education on innovative structural designs. Auto mechanics familiar with one kind of car could wear augmented reality glasses when learning how to repair cars of a different make. Almost any kind of diagnostic work could be enhanced with augmented reality.

Think about how significant augmented reality will be in education. Children going on field trips will have much more knowledge and information. Curiosity can be immediately satisfied, and self-directed learning can happen anywhere. Adults wanting to learn a new profession or skill may not need to spend a lot of time and money to go back to school. Instead they can wear the augmented reality glasses or goggles of their new profession, like the auto mechanic mentioned above, and learn the skills that are immediately needed. In other words, augmented reality will not only enhance learning experiences at all levels, it may in fact replace some forms of education at lower costs and allow people to complete it in less time. Augmented reality will allow self-directed learning to accelerate, as it can take place anywhere. Those that want to move more quickly, and therefore less expensively, through higher education can do so. In addition, augmented reality will allow classroom time to be much more about high-level conceptual interaction, as data and facts can be instantly accessed before, during, and after the time in the classroom. The essential technical skills taught in community colleges and trade schools can be learned more deeply and quickly and can be applied immediately at jobs students are working while obtaining their degree.

The second level of transformation with augmented reality could occur when it is applied to people. Wearing augmented glasses, you might be able to look at someone of interest and quickly know as much about them as is known by anyone else in the world. This would be taking what people now do with social media—learning about and understanding someone by taking a look at his/her online profile—to a whole new level. Just think of the conversation on the first date between two people wearing augmented reality glasses. No one will ever ask "What's your sign?" again!

When will all this happen? Probably in the next ten years, or less! As of the writing of this book in 2012, there are many augmented reality apps available for smartphones, and Google has announced and previewed augmented reality glasses to be available in 2013.[4] Augmented reality will change behavior and disrupt many social "norms." It is hard to imagine an area of society or business that will not be affected by this merging of information, knowledge, and reality.

This is one of the technologies that will define the Shift Age.

## TRULY AUTOMATIC AUTOMOBILES

In 2012 we are seeing the beginnings of the driverless car. Google has focused a lot of research, time, energy, and testing into the development of a car that is driven solely by a computer.[5] Other companies are working on similar initiatives as well. The driverless car will soon be a reality.

Many of us have experienced the high-tech cars of today that show us the view behind the car when backing up or give us directions when we have made a wrong turn on our way to a selected destination. This technology will combine with deeper computer intelligence to take over the driving of the car fully from humans.

How will fully automatic cars benefit our society? The computer-driven car will dramatically cut down on accidents and highway fatalities. It will become the designated driver. It will allow one to work or sleep while in motion. It will allow one to text, email, conduct a meeting, or watch a video, all while moving from one place to another.

The technology, safety, and efficiency of the driverless car will be developed much more quickly than it will be able to be widely utilized due to all the incredibly slow-moving government bureaucracies that will insert their slow approvals into the process. As discussed earlier, the governmental parts of society move much more slowly than the rest of society. There will be a good deal of fear about allowing driverless cars to be on the highways. Humanity has never experienced cars that did not have a person behind the steering wheel, so the truly automatic automobile is a paradigm shift that will take time to be accepted. That said, the first cars truly worthy of the name "automatic" will become mainstream in the Shift Age.

## THREE-DIMENSIONAL PRINTING AND CUSTOM MANUFACTURING

The definition of manufacturing is about to change. The twentieth century defined manufacturing largely in "mass" terminology: mass production, economies of scale, lowest-cost mass production. In the twenty-first century and starting now in the Shift Age, there is a new definition clearly in sight: custom manufacturing through 3D printing.

Three-dimensional printing from digital designs is about to become widespread. The technology has been in development with prototypes for a number of years, and it is now about to become cost-effective and scalable.

This new means of production values innovation, quality, and customization over quantity. Creativity and innovation now lead as opposed to cheap labor and volume. This means that countries and cultures that are at the high end of the innovation scale can compete with those at the low

Three-dimensional printing works by building layer upon layer of deposited materials to create single objects. These high-tech printers will use a variety of materials from plastics to metals to create on a small scale and at much lower investment levels. In the future, 3D printing will make it possible to produce individual items as cheaply as tens of thousands, on a per-unit basis. So manufacturing finally will become cost effective at the custom level.

end of the cost scale. The worldview of industrial production is about to change significantly in the next fifteen to twenty years.

Another way to think about it is that it is a new industrial revolution. Custom manufacturing, the "new industrial revolution," is aligned with the Earth Century and the need to view our planet as Spaceship Earth. Excess production of goods will be a memory. We will move into an era when there will be fewer manufacturing overruns that create surplus quantities of products that will not be used. We will create only what we need rather than producing volumes of stuff we don't need.

The industrial revolution of the Digital Age is now here. This trend of custom manufacturing will be driven in part by ever more sophisticated and widespread implementation of nanotechnology.

## NANOTECHNOLOGY

A nanometer is a billionth of a meter. Nanotechnology is therefore working at the atomic or molecular level. A human hair is approximately 100,000 nanometers in width. To put it in perspective, the common cliché used to explain the size of a nanometer is that a nanometer is to a meter what a marble is to Earth. It is generally accepted in 2012 that working on anything that is 100 nanometers or less is the realm of nanotechnology.

Nanotechnology is already transforming many industries. Production, manufacturing, and health care are all being profoundly affected by it. The ability to create and produce at this molecular level is already influencing computer chip design. It is creating new materials and altering the quality of existing materials. This will be one of the first significant market outcomes of nanotechnology: adding qualities or improving qualities of existing materials at the molecular level. The initial, low-level use of nano-technology was to make clothing stain resistant.

Inevitably, nanotechnology will move us into that major context of biology and technology merging. It will be one of the technologies leading us to redefine the terms "man made" and "life," and it will do this before the Transformation Decade is over.

## ROBOTS

Robots have always been the poster children of the future. Robots have populated science fiction as the non-humans or the mechanical humanoids. We have a well-developed, Hollywood-influenced anthropomorphic vision of what they will look and act like. While that will of course become reality, there will be many other aspects in the now exploding field of robotics that will also transform humanity. Currently, there are widely available robots that clean floors and perform precision work on assembly lines

Manufacturing has already been transformed and will continue to be. An increasing amount of manual labor will become robotic. Health care will have widespread use of robotics—the young and particularly the elderly will have a lot of time interfacing with robots: the young, because they will grow up with robots; and the elderly, because they will be helped and monitored by them at home. There will be hidden robotics in much of what we buy or interact with in the years ahead.

There will be, perhaps not until the 2020s, a field of robotics that will create companions for humans just as in those science fiction novels and movies we have consumed. Is it real or is it a robot? In the Shift Age, the science fiction view of robots will start to become a reality. As with all the other developments around the merging of biology and technology, this will come up against some legacy morality. Robotics, as a field, as an industry, as a force in society, is here and in a rapid state of development.

As robots move more toward human work and human behavior, so humans will increasingly have more technology in our bodies with bionics.

## BIONICS

As discussed in the Health and Medicine chapter, bionics will play an increasing role. Bionics will alter the body, extend life, create freedom of movement for the handicapped, and provide people the possibility to live better, longer lives—lives that, without bionics, they could not experience.

Quadriplegics could be walking down the street by 2015. In that same year, artificial eyeballs could be implanted to provide 20/20 eyesight with a ten-year warranty. Limbs with superior functionality and strength could replace the limb lost at war on in an accident. In other words, we will very soon have replacement parts that will be superior to what we were born with. This is one of the reasons I tell people over the age of forty to try to stay in really good shape and in good health. If you can be healthy in the year 2025, you will have the chance to live years longer than expected, due in part to superior replacement parts.

The leading-edge work today, which means in the wider market by 2015, is the integration of bionics with brainwaves. The brain can remember the thoughts that instructed a hand or a limb to perform a certain movement. When a limb is lost, the brain still has that memory, so when a new bionic arm is attached, it will be sophisticated enough to get connected to the neurological passageways to the brain so the brain can control it. Neurological integration of bionic parts with the body: that is transformational.

Bionics will initially be this clear technological incursion into the human body, and that is the way I am using the word here. The question in the next few years is whether the live tissue we will start to create in the laboratory via genetic breakthroughs will be considered bionics or something completely different. In 2012, the use of the word clearly implies non-tissue implants. In the years ahead, tissue regeneration or creation will be considered either bionics or something else. I leave this semantic discussion for others.

The Transformation Decade, 2010–2020, will be the first full decade of widespread bionics.

## VOICE RECOGNITION AND TRANSLATION SOFTWARE

Voice recognition software is now widely used in developed nations. We use it to dictate texts and emails on computers and phones. We use it to speak to artificial intelligence companions on smartphones. This technology has developed incredibly fast in just the last few years. In 2009, dictating emails was at best a mediocre experience. Three years later, in 2012, the accuracy of this software is exponentially better. Take this steep slope of improvement and cast it forward into the future.

For much of the early twenty-first century, good and functional keyboards have been a continuing liability of app phones and tablets. In the Transformation Decade, this will no longer be the case. Imagine most if not all of your short communications such as email and texts being spoken rather than written. This of course will only increase the move to mobile computing as keyboards become optional. Some people will still use keyboards; others will leave them behind, similar to the time when some people continued to use slide rules when calculators came to market. There will be choice. By 2015, there will be early discussion about whether keyboards will be obsolete—they won't be. By 2020, the conversation in K–12 education will be whether we need to continue to teach keyboarding, similar to the discussions going on in that space today about needing to continue to teach cursive writing.

I can imagine a day when one of you reading these words will speak to a grandchild about using a keyboard and she will say "Grandma, what's a keyboard?"

Now, combine voice recognition software with language translation software, and we have a transformation. We will no longer need to learn foreign languages, unless we choose to. Certainly by 2015, if not earlier, it will be reality that we will have highly accurate voice-activated language translation apps on our phones. An American going to China will purchase the Chinese language app before the trip. Want to find the Apple store in Shanghai? Just speak into your phone that query in English and the phone will ask the question in Chinese. Think about that!

In the years ahead, language translation software, combined with voice recognition software, can be downloaded onto any computer. This means that if you want to have a video conference on your computer—or mobile device—with someone who speaks a different language, you can, with only the short lag time for translation.

By 2020, the learning of a foreign language will only be an activity to do as neuroscience shows that brain development is enhanced by learning a foreign language. Or it might take on the cachet of scholarship, such as being able to speak Latin has today—a sign of education if not practicality. The necessity of learning a foreign language will have been largely removed by this technological development. Technology will, to a great degree, allow us to bridge the language barriers we have lived with our entire history.

## BRAINWAVE COMPUTER INTERFACE

Today, in 2012, there are the early-stage developments of brainwave computer interface technology. This technology will experience incredible growth in the next few years, resulting in profound changes in many areas of society.

All of us have brainwaves. To simplify a bit, they are the electrical impulses of our brains that translate into thoughts. So brainwave mapping is the mapping of our thoughts. This technology has come from several sources. A primary application is the use of reading brainwaves for quadriplegics to move their high-tech wheelchairs. "Rotate wheelchair right," and the wheelchair turns right. "Move wheelchair forward," and the wheelchair moves forward.

It is this technology that is now available today for a few hundred dollars. It is the first, very basic iteration, with limited capability. One puts on a headset with a variable number of brainwave sensors, and the software program asks you to think about certain things. Once the brainwaves of those thoughts are captured, then you can look at a computer screen and, when prompted by the on-screen avatar to do something, you think it and it happens on the screen.

Brainwave computer interface is the next human interface with computer technology, following the current iteration of touch and voice. Remember, just a few short years ago, one had to type when interfacing with a computing device. It was the only way to interface with any type of computer. Now touch and voice interfaces are common.

The potential of this new technology is stunning almost beyond comprehension. A metaphor for the sophistication of brainwave technology in 2012 versus 2020 might be the comparison of the Pong video game of the 1970s with video games today. We are now in liftoff mode.

Think about the level of concentration we can and will quickly develop when doing brainwave interface with computers. This will quickly become the antidote to the development of distracted, short-attention-span states of mind in these digital ages.

Think about video games. By 2015, there should be video games that will be played by having the gamer wear a brainwave headset that can capture the unique way he thinks about, say, pulling a trigger or turning to the left or any other move of a first shooter type of game. After benchmarking his brainwaves, he can play the game with just that head—without a hand-held controller! Think about the competitive levels of concentration that one will develop when playing someone else. Start to think about what happened last night—boom! You just got shot by your opponent as your mind wandered.

Think about education and all that can occur. As I mentioned in the education chapter, how will we be teaching a fourteen-year-old middle school student in the classroom when she is doing two hours of brainwave interface in the home? Think how the Digital Natives will take to this so much more naturally than their elders.

Now, on the highest level of the Shift Age, think about the coming evolutionary shift in consciousness discussed in Chapter Thirteen. After having ten years of brainwave interface with a computer, will it not be easier to make this next evolutionary step up? I think that brainwave technology will lead to other, even more transformative technologies ahead (see the next section).

# Transformative Technologies of the Future
## ATMOSPHERIC CLEANSING

In the global discussion about climate change, the emphasis has been on the need to slow the massive release of $CO_2$ into the atmosphere that began with the Industrial Age and greatly accelerated in the last quarter of the twentieth century. This very valid discussion has led to the general conclusion that humanity needs to lessen its consumption of fossil fuels and do so soon. However, until now, the discussion about climate change, global warming and dramatically increasing levels of $CO_2$ has basically been a supply-side, cause-driven discussion.

We are now moving into the next stage of this discussion, which is the "cleansing, removal" discussion. What absorbs $CO_2$ better than anything else on the planet? Trees and plants. So, stated simply, one of the most important transformative technologies of the future is to create something that outperforms the tree. Create something that absorbs $CO_2$ from the atmosphere in a similar way to a tree, from the surrounding atmosphere. Humanity has been increasing $CO_2$ at rates faster than the planet's plants can absorb it, so simply planting more trees will not be the solution, as all the trees in the world are losing the battle. There has been some early success with coating buildings with titanium dioxide, a whitening agent that seems to absorb $CO_2$ from the immediate air surrounding the building.[6] There are other chemical agents that in early-stage development have promise. The issue with this is that, at best, it is a defensive measure, similar to the planting of a tree. If the amount of $CO_2$ in the atmosphere was static and not increasing, or was in fact declining, this level of technology would perhaps be enough. But the amount of $CO_2$ is increasing, so this will not be enough.

The transformative technology that might well come along within the next few years would go beyond the tree model and move to the "vacuum cleaner" model: actively sucking $CO_2$ particulates out of the atmosphere. This is an environmentalist's holy grail technology. It will be developed during the Shift Age. The question is when it can be scaled up to a global level of impact so that this technology can actually overcompensate for the $CO_2$ humanity is putting into the atmosphere. This could well happen by the 2020s, and if so might be one of the more influential technologies of the Earth Century, of the Anthropocene Era.

## HOLOGRAPHIC COMMUNICATION DEVICES

Hand-held devices will become ever more powerful in the coming years. The functionality of these devices will continue to increase as well. The recent past is a clear guide to that directional trend.

The next wave of such transformation is rapidly approaching.

One of the clear developments will be holographic projection and communication devices that bring our interactions into 3D. Instead of video images on screens, there will be holographic interactions with team members or dancing with your loved one who is on the other side of the world. We all remember *Star Wars*, right?

This holographic technology is now showing up in select concert situations with expensive reflection devices. Holography will most likely start very large and very expensive, and therefore its availability and uses will be limited and selective—the same as the seventy-five-year history of the computer, only on a much more abbreviated time table. Then it will become a two-way communication technology, again very expensive and limited. Then technological transformation will kick in, so that by 2020 we will be able to carry holographic communication capability with us.

## SECOND-GENERATION AUGMENTED REALITY

The second generation of augmented reality will kick in when other technologies get invented that can approximate the physical reality relative to the senses. When these technologies are blended into the then-sophisticated augmented reality technology of that future day, well, the imagination runs wild. It will be the stage of actually "jacking in" to an altered reality.

As with several of these transformative technologies, second-generation augmented reality will further alter the way we think about reality, relationships, sex, travel, work, and religion. This of course means that there will be a lot of resistance to it, as it will confront "established" legacy thinking, some of it centuries old.

This will be a partial merging of the physical and screen realities that will have been transforming at significantly different rates. This means that the technological possibilities will be ahead of the place-based thinking of the physical place to which they are introduced. We will be in a physical place but will be taken to such a fully multi-sensorial space that while our biological processes will be in one place, our neurological and sensory processes will be of another space.

It is hard to imagine, as the potential and possibilities transcend how any individual perceives them. Want to spend time on a wonderful beach for an hour every day? You can. Want to have intimate relations with the sexual partner of your dreams? You can. Want to listen to Einstein talk and be able to ask him questions? You can. The developed level of this technology will be such that all of these examples will be recalled by the self and the brain as actually having been experienced. This is a true merging of real and not real, of real and the highest level of augmentation. From a social point of view, this has the highest levels of both fun and danger inherent in it. Some will use this technology to simply "check out." Others will use it to truly deepen their life experience. This is no different from the technology called a book. Some people read them to escape. Others read them to deepen their knowledge.

## COLLECTIVE CONSCIOUSNESS INTERFACE TECHNOLOGY

This one is a bit hard to truly comprehend. I do believe it will happen sometime in the 2020s. This technological forecast is based upon my earlier metaphor that the current, rapidly expanding, synaptic cyberspace called the Neurosphere is a technological model for a new evolutionary shift in consciousness that looks likely to occur in the 2020s. I base this time frame upon the current rate and acceleration of change and the clear change in consciousness and awareness that has occurred in recent years and seems to be accelerating as well.

So the prediction here is that once this new, collective level of consciousness begins to become widely manifested, a technology will be created to assist those yet to deeply experience it. It might be something like a hand-held tablet with earphones, or more likely something that gently covers the head. This cover might contain both the highest level of brainwave sensors and some inbound antenna that truly can operate at the delicate frequency of, and sense, others' brainwaves.

This is an accelerative technology of the absolute highest order. Helping more people to connect into this elevated, collective next evolutionary stage of human consciousness has consequences that one can only theorize about here in 2012. This technology takes us into deep metaphysical, spiritual, philosophical, and moral areas where consciousness expands and becomes adaptive. *Evolutionary* is the right word.

# CHAPTER SEVENTEEN

# ENERGY

Energy is and will be one of the most important issues for human-ity in the Shift Age. This is no different than any of the prior ages. Energy has always been important, as it is the lifeblood of society. It has always been prized, and has created great wealth, as it is essential to the functioning of the economy. With the move from the Agricultural to the Industrial Age and the discovery and use of fossil fuels, energy became a primary ingredient of economic growth and the glories of all that has hap-pened in the last 200 years.

Hundreds of books have been written about energy, different sources of energy, and the solutions to change what is clearly a dangerous situation with energy relative to Earth. Many of these books have been written by some of the smartest energy experts and scientists alive today. As a futurist I embrace all the great thinking that is being brought to the field of energy in the early part of this century. As a futurist I look to how humanity must navigate this time in its history of energy use. Therefore, this chapter only speaks to the high-level conceptual conversation that must be had as we fully enter the Shift Age.

## Twentieth-Century Energy

Energy, along with the explosive growth in population, was one of the reasons that more wealth was created in the twentieth century than in all history before. Energy fuels wealth creation.

Think of all the inventions of the twentieth century mentioned earlier. Many of them created new, growing needs for energy. Be it electricity, the internal combustion engine, airplanes, or suburbia, much of what was invented was based upon some source of energy. The economic expansion and increase in the standard of living around the world since World War II was to a large degree based upon energy, access to energy, and lowering the costs of producing and using energy.

Now we have a problem. Fossil fuel usage has clearly changed the amount of $CO_2$ in the atmosphere and is affecting the planet. This has led to the development of alternative energy sources such as hydro, wind, solar, biofuels, and geothermal. These alternative and renewable sources of energy have started to reach scalable levels in recent years. This makes them not only an increasing part of the overall energy mix but ever more price competitive to fossil fuels.

Recently, there has been an explosive growth in the supply of natural gas with an accompanying collapse in price. This fossil fuel will increase dramatically in usage in the next few years, replacing other more expensive and less environmentally friendly fuels such as coal and petroleum.[1] All fossil fuels give off $CO_2$, but natural gas does so at lower levels than coal or petroleum. The energy needs of humanity will require that all these fossil fuels must be utilized. That said, the push toward alternative and renewable energy sources will result in lower prices and greater use.

This means that in the Transformation Decade, and accelerating in the 2020s, the percentage of energy generated that is from fossil fuels will decline.

By 2020, the overall percentage of total global energy consumption that comes from fossil fuels will be much less than today.

For the past few years, I have suggested to audiences all over the world that the single greatest wealth opportunity in human history could be in the areas of alternative and renewable energy. There could be more money to be made than has been made in the computing industry to date. There are 2 billion people who have computers but more than 6 billion people who directly or indirectly consume fossil fuels every day.[2] Fossil fuels will only decline as a percentage of energy consumed, as the readily available supplies of them decrease. The innovators, inventors, and creators of replacements for fossil fuel can and will make incredible amounts of money. This is a good thing in a largely capitalistic world. The obvious effect of these coming innovations and breakthroughs will be both a lessening of the $CO_2$ that is released into the atmosphere and a lessening dependence on what is ultimately a finite resource of fossil fuels. The United States represents 5 percent of the world's population but consumes 25 percent of the energy produced in the world. If all of humanity consumed fossil fuels at the level of the United States, it would take four earths to provide the fossil fuel to do so. If the history of energy of the last 150 years has been fossil fuels, the history of energy for the next 150 years will be about their replacements.

## A Systemic Global View

As we move into the Shift Age, the global discussion around energy must change. It must change from the recent, limited focus on energy sources and finding replacements for them to a larger, more integrated global view. There is no single answer relative to energy sources. It is an "all of the above" situation for the next decade. All current sources of energy will be utilized. Alternative and renewable sources will grow as a percentage of the whole, but will still be only a part of global energy consumption.

It is clear that the thinking about energy will move from being industry-specific and nation-specific to being global. We must start to discuss global energy in a systemic way. All forms of energy, old and new, will move toward a blended whole that acknowledges the economic, climatic, and social realities now facing humanity.

Rather than make low-level arguments for this source or that source of energy, we need to elevate our energy vision to a much more systemic approach that looks at sources, locations, and consumption patterns through a global lens. Only at this level can we navigate humanity's energy future. To use a couple of phrases from R. Buckminster Fuller, we must now have a "design revolution" and utilize "comprehensive anticipatory design science" to design the vision for global energy for the remainder of the twenty-first century.

In other words, we need to start to look at energy from an integrated global perspective. We have to develop an intelligent, cohesive vision and plan to move the world forward to a new energy age of ever less fossil fuel. How can we do this?

> We first have to take a look at the known and projected amounts of energy in the world.
>> How many known resources of fossil fuels are there in the world?
>> What is the 2012 level of hydroelectric, solar, wind, geothermal, and biofuel energy generation, and what will the growth of each of these be over the next ten years?
> Then we have to look at where all these energy resources and sources are and where they are currently consumed.
> We also need to look at which areas or nations are on their way to energy independence, those with the highest percentage of alternative and renewable energy usage.

The goal is first to create a global availability view, then a global consumption view, and finally to map the areas that can most quickly move to alternative and renewable. Once this is achieved, we can map the greatest amounts of energy waste and drive efficiency and conservation in those areas.

The Global Council is an arbitrary name I have given to what I see as an inevitable global organization that comes into being, initially on an issue-by-issue basis, to deal with the global issues that transcend nation-states and the United Nations.

How can this be done? This may be one of the primary issues—along with the related climate change issue—that initiates the movement toward the Global Council idea set forth in Chapter Three.

Energy is fundamentally now a global issue, as its use affects all of us globally. Global entities will be created initially around issues or problems that have largely global solutions. Climate change and a cohesive long-term vision for humanity's use of energy calls out for the creation of a global entity that comes from the Spaceship Earth point of view rather than any nation-state's self-interest. This new energy council will be initially a design entity that will work on the systemic design of global energy development and use, with global support, to entirely recast the view of energy and humanity. When energy use in one part of the world affects another part of the world, which is where we now are, this becomes the necessity.

> One might think of the Global Council on Energy as the most intelligent, connected chat room about energy. It would consist of leading thinkers and visionaries charged with the task of global systems design for human energy use in the Earth Century.

# Retrofitting the Use of Energy

The concept that most affects the future of energy for the next twenty years is retrofitting the twentieth century. The landscape most of us live in was shaped by the energy and transportation inventions of the twentieth century. We now see this landscape as of its time, wasteful, not sustainable, and therefore in need of significant retrofitting for the twenty-first century. We have more than tripled in number since the internal combustion engine vehicle came to market. We live in this landscape that is based on assumptions of many fewer people, much lower costs, infinite supply, and high levels of waste.

We are not only stuck in the legacy thinking about energy from the last century, we are locked down in the vast, wasteful landscape it created. In Chapter Ten, Retrofitting the Twentieth Century was defined as one of the five major contexts of the Shift Age. As we envision, design, and implement the retrofitting of the twentieth century, integrating intelligent use—and reuse—of energy will be central to the design of the twenty-first-century human landscape. In order to do so, it will be essential to let go of what was cast in the last century as the benchmark for this century. Since so much of infrastructure in the world today is crumbling and in disrepair, why not use this opportunity to fully think what replacement for it should be? What might a viable energy infrastructure that will serve humanity in 2050 look like?

As we face the huge task of retrofitting the twentieth century, it is the ideal time to fully integrate a completely new, integrated view of energy. This new, integrated view of energy will incorporate:

» new electric grids that are more efficient and integrated
» a complementary designed implementation of non-distributed energy sources from variable energy sources that can be stored with new battery technologies
» a completely rethought view of a transportation infrastructure that is something beyond the current one, which is fundamentally based upon the internal combustion engine
» a global mandate for roofs to be green gardens, painted white with reflective and $CO_2$-capturing titanium dioxide or other such coatings, solar capture surfaces, and rain retention systems
» a commitment to efficiency with implementation of smart technologies into the grids
» a high-speed, low-cost wireless grid to move society to ever more online economic activity and interaction, lessening the dependency on energy-intensive transportation

# Twenty-First-Century Energy Breakthroughs

As this new global infrastructure and energy use design vision is being created, there are a number of developments that have great promise in 2012:

» new battery and storage technologies for long-term storage of variable energy

» new generations of nuclear power plants that are smaller and more efficient and utilize ever smaller amounts of radioactive fuel

» more efficient and lower-cost solar capture systems that can literally be painted on surfaces with built-in connectivity for immediate use or storage

» a breakthrough in fusion technologies

» alternative forms of personal transportation vehicles that do not run on fossil fuels and are cost competitive

» the economically efficient utilization of nature's energy from solar, wind, waves, and geothermal sources in both distributed and non-distributed ways

The global energy vision, 2012–2040, must be seen through the lenses of the Earth Century and Spaceship Earth. It is this century that is the time. It is this, the only known planet that is home to humanity, that is our tiny, precious spaceship.

# CHAPTER EIGHTEEN

# MEDICINE AND HEALTH MANAGEMENT

M edicine and health care will be transformed in the Shift Age. The New Health Age has just begun, in which humanity has entered a new age of health just as we enter the Shift Age. In this chapter we look at the fundamental changes about to occur and the medical miracles that are around the corner in this New Health Age.

Health care and medicine are relatively recent in the 150,000-year timespan of modern humanity. The first mention of either was in 4500 B.C. in ancient Babylonia.[1] Modern medicine, measured from the discovery of germs, is only about 150 years old. Today in 2012, we stand on a threshold of a new age in medicine and health care.

In the book *The New Health Age: The Future of Health Care in America*, published in early 2012, my coauthor Jonathan Fleece and I wrote about this new age of health and medicine with an orientation to the United States. The analysis we made in that book and the research that we did for is still current and accurate today, so I feel it's important to reiterate the developed thinking from that book. While the United States is at the beginning of an entirely new stage in health care thinking, delivery, and economic models, there is much global consistency to the fundamentals of the New Health Age.

## Medical Miracles around the Corner

As discussed in earlier chapters that examined the merging of biology and technology and technological advances, new technologies are coming to the marketplace that are affecting and will affect medicine. In addition, there are social forces and infrastructure developments that will also effect great change. Here is a list of what will change the face of medicine, just in the current Transformation Decade:

» Human life span on the rise—Life expectancy in the developed countries of the world increased by 50 percent in the twentieth century. People born in 1900 had an average life expectancy of fifty years at birth. By 2000, that average had increased to seventy-five years. This increase was more than that of the 3,000 years prior. Numerous medical thinkers, researchers, and scientists think there might be that same percentage increase in the next fifteen years! This means that someone born in a developed country in 2025 could have a life expectancy of 100 years or more. This means that many of the children of the Shift Age Generations will be alive into the twenty-second century. There is a small but growing group of scientists and thinkers that look at aging as something that can be cured. Think about that: aging as a treatable condition!

» Low-cost genetic mapping—It took more than $300 million dollars over thirteen years to fully map the human genome by 2003. By the year 2015 if not sooner, it's highly probable that any individual will be able to have their entire genetic map done for $1,000 or less. This will transform health care. Think about being a twenty-five-year-old woman in 2015 whose genetic map shows the reality of early onset of Alzheimer's. What would she do? She would go into active disease prevention mode to do whatever might lower her risk of developing it. Genetic mapping will allow us to use preventive measures to manage our own genetics. The knowledge that we have a genetic disposition for a disease or condition can be known in advance and can therefore be anticipated and perhaps treated.

» DNA pharmaceuticals—Instead of using the current lowest-common-denominator drugs of today, with all their long lists of side effects and with sometimes iffy treatment results, we will begin to develop and use specific, targeted, and personalized pharmaceuticals.

» Bionics—Bionics is here and will rapidly grow in complexity with ever more integration into our neurological systems. In this New Health Age, for the first time in history, many of our replacement parts will be superior to those that we were born with.

» Robotics—Robotics will impact medicine and health care in three ways. First, it will allow for technical life improvement with such things as exoskeletons for paraplegics and quadriplegics. Second, it will greatly expand surgical capabilities by providing greater exactness and more microscopic precision than the human hand. Third, it will help to lower health care costs for the aged, by providing assistance and monitoring in the home.

» Tissue regeneration—Currently in laboratories around the world there has been significant success and progress in the regeneration of human tissue. Scientists have successfully regenerated fingers and such internal organs as bladders. Think about the true possibility of having your heart regenerated if you know from your genetic map that you have a high risk of heart disease. You will have a replacement heart ready. These early successes will spread in scope and degree.

» Human cloning—In the last two decades, humans have successfully cloned animals. These breakthroughs, combined with tissue regeneration, point to the real possibility of cloning humans in the next decade. This leads to the discussion about the definition of life. What if your loved one is dying? Might you not want to clone him so that you could continue a life with him? Would he still be himself? It also will confront us with the moral dilemma of what to do with the failed efforts along the way. Cloning may never become socially, morally, or legally acceptable, but the science will be successfully developed.

» Creation of artificial life—As discussed in Chapter Twelve about the merging of biology with technology, this one is a science just beginning and with great implications for health care and society. We might well soon have ways to generate life as yet unknown in 2012. This of course will raise huge moral issues.

» Socially engineered health—This is taking our knowledge of health and embedding it into our education, culture, habits, and infrastructures. Think about the fact that we all know that walking is good for us, but that there are suburban communities that have no sidewalks. In the Shift Age, when we are retrofitting the twentieth century and creating smart cities, humanity will design its new landscape with the intention of maximizing health.

» Connectivity—Increasingly, global health care systems will use connectivity to bring efficiency and lower costs. In 2012, less than 30 percent of all medical records are digital or electronic. Compare that with any other industry. In 2012, we all regularly go online to research major purchases before making them. That is something we cannot do with the non-connected, opaque health care system. When was the last time you could compare price and performance about a car online? Perhaps yesterday. Are you able to do that for a hip replacement surgery? Not today. Simply put, all the connectivity we expect in the rest of the economy is coming soon to health care. Rather than going into the doctor's office when not feeling well, you can dial into the office via a video Skype–type service to interact with a health care professional. This would be after taking your own various vital signs with your mobile devices. Then, in the Era of Big Data discussed in Chapter Twelve, your personal data would be compared to that of all the people who had the same symptoms in the prior year. So the technical and connective world will more fully enter the world of medicine and health care.[2]

A general way to look at these coming medical miracles is to realize that it is very important, particularly to people over forty reading this book, to stay as healthy as possible until 2025. By 2025, I forecast that there will so many new miracles in medicine that the possibility of living decades longer will become a reality for many.

# Dynamic Flows

In our book *The New Health Age: The Future of Health Care in America*, Jonathan Fleece and I realized that the forces and dynamics of change in health care in the United States and globally could be grouped into three categories: how we think about health care, how we deliver health care, and the economics of health care. In all cases humanity is moving from the left side to the right side of each of these nine dynamic flows.

## HOW HUMANITY THINK WILL THINK ABOUT HEALTH CARE

Sickness → Wellness

Ignorance → Awareness/Understanding

Opposition → Alignment

## HOW HEALTH CARE WILL BE DELIVERED

Treatment → Prevention

Reactive → Proactive

Episodic → Holistic

## THE NEW ECONOMICS OF HEALTH CARE

Procedures → Performance

Isolation → Integration

Inefficient → Efficient

The way to understand what global health care will be like in the Shift Age is to look at these nine dynamic flows and realize that, on varying timelines, all nations will be moving to the right side of these flows. One of the primary reasons is that health care costs around the world have gone up dramatically in the last two decades. The preceding flows, to varying degrees, all will help to lower health care costs. A second major reason is that the human cost of prevention and being proactive is much lower than waiting until treatment. Focusing on being healthy will produce greater well-being than waiting until people are sick to treat them. Finally, the Shift Age will be a time of great migration, so being able to connect to one's medical records from anywhere in the world will be increasingly important.

# Health Management

If you look at the right side of all the flows, you will see that global health is becoming more preventive, connected, and based upon managing one's health preventatively rather than in the reactive treatment of one's illnesses. In the Shift Age "health care" will give way to "health management." The connectivity, digitalization, and global market price transparency so prevalent in other segments of society and economics will become central to health management. No matter where you are in the world, you will be able to have your entire medical record both on your person and accessible from the Cloud.

The Shift Age will be a time of ever greater health, longer life, and deeper knowledge of the brain and genetics, and a time when we all can become more in control of our health and well-being.

# CHAPTER NINETEEN

# EDUCATION

The Shift Age will be a truly transformational time for education and will see probably the greatest amount of change in the shortest amount of time in the history of education. All levels of education will be transformed, from pre-school through graduate school. Long-held structures and traditions, decades and even centuries old, will be wiped away by a tsunami of transformative change.

Let us first take a look at each of the levels of education and how they will change in the Shift Age.

## Pre-School

The changes at this level will be driven by two significant dynamics.

The first is that, by definition, the children moving through this level will all be part of the second wave of Digital Natives, those born 2009 and after. They will enter kindergarten and nursery school with some level of digital skills and experience. Many three- to five-year-olds will have had significant experience using app phones and tablets. They will have spent hundreds of hours experiencing screen reality before their first day at nursery school. Consequently, they will expect connectivity in the classroom and will have developed habits and a greater desire for immediacy of interaction. This will have to be addressed in ways currently not present today. Pre-school is still largely the analog environment it has been for decades. As discussed in Chapter Fourteen, this second wave of Digital Natives will have experienced interaction screens since before they could talk. This is an entirely different generation of children than has ever entered pre-school.

The second, and potentially much more significant development is the possibility of incorporating or applying new knowledge about early childhood brain development into pre-school. We have learned more about the brain development of infants in the last decade than in all the time before. Why not assimilate this into pre-school education around the world? More has been learned about the brain in the field of neuroscience in the last two decades than in all history. We are much more knowledgeable about how the brain develops in the first years of life than we ever have been before. Think about how much that knowledge might affect how we could accelerate learning in children three to five years old.

The single most profound statement I have ever heard about the integration of neuroscience into education was from a good friend of mine, Dr. Jim Rex. At the time Jim was the Secretary of Education for the State of South Carolina, responsible for K–12 education for the entire state. In mid-2009 Jim convened a two-day conference on the future of education for the state.

At this level of schooling, much of the educational value is in children's developing social interaction skills for the first time. How to share, how to play together, how to express themselves, and how to find their place in this first area of social interaction will still remain key to their ability to successfully navigate society in the future, regardless of their individual levels of digital development. However, the issue that will need to be addressed is that these second-wave Digital Natives will have both earlier and greater levels of synaptic activity going on in their brains than prior generations due to the time spent with digital devices. To socialize these children and create a positive first experience of education and school, educators must fully embrace the highly interactive touchscreen realities that these children are experiencing outside the classroom. To not embrace connectivity in the classroom may intentionally or inadvertently create a first impression that being in school is being in isolated non-connectedness.

Luminaries such as Richard Riley, former governor of South Carolina and former Secretary of Education for the United States, were in attendance. I was honored to be the keynote speaker.

At the end of the conference, Jim offered up some closing comments. During these comments he leaned into the microphone and said:

> If we incorporated all that we have learned in the last twenty years about the development of the brain from the day of birth through age five and brought it into our early childhood education, we could change this country in a generation.

In the Shift Age we have the opportunity for the first time to integrate the incredible knowledge we are learning daily in the field of neuroscience into the education of our young.

# K–12

In 2011, *Shift Ed: A Call to Action for Transforming K–12 Education*, my friend and coauthor Jeff Cobb and I called for nothing less that transformation of education at this level. Transformation is the only way. Reform is too little, too late. The way we think about the school year, the school day, the way students can move as quickly as they want through subject matter, and the connected technology increasingly available to all will largely alter the thinking and therefore the landscape of K–12 education in the United States and around the world.

Since the spring of 2011, I have travelled the United States speaking to K–12 educators at the national, state, and district levels. I speak to a vision of transformation to challenge them to follow it or create their own. What is so incredibly exciting is that educators are stepping into the process with relish. Legacy thinking is now being challenged. As we wrote in the book, there is a phase transition taking

A prime example of a phase transition is water. At 211 degrees it is water but a liquid; at 212 it is water but steam.

place, a school and a district at a time. True transformative leadership and change is probably still at the single-digit level in terms of number of schools, but I feel that by 2015 it will be well into double digits.

School superintendents everywhere are simply initiating transformation. They are asking themselves and their staffs challenging questions. They are engaging school boards and civic leaders to stand with them for transformation. They are simply changing technologies and initiating cloud computing for schools. To witness the direction and speed of transformation in K–12 education, it is only necessary to travel across the country to see some of the ways superintendents are implementing transformative leadership.

Dr. Karen Woodward, Superintendent of the Lexington One school district in South Carolina—who wrote a change vision for *Shift Ed*—has provided an iPad to each of the 8,000 high school students in her district and is working to extend that to middle school. This increases collaboration, lowers textbook costs, and accelerates a learning process more in tune with highly interactive touchscreen life in the Shift Age. She has her school board working closely with her, as the changes are palpable and measurable, essential qualities. I met with most of her school board, and they are completely involved with helping Dr. Woodward implement change. Dr. Woodward is a prime example of the essential need to have the Superintendent be in a close, dynamic, and collaborative relationship with the school board.

Dr. Eric Williams, Superintendent of the York County Division in Virginia, is creating a transformative technology infrastructure. As Eric said to me over a delightful dinner, "We want students to leverage technology to connect globally with peers and adults." To do so he is creating a 24/7 cloud with high-speed bandwidth and access in the district that additionally allows for virtual learning, creating a blended learning approach that will be integral to Shift Age education on all levels. This allows students both to move forward at varying rates and to comfortably integrate the screen and physical realities they have already adapted to outside the classroom. An extension of this is to encourage students to bring, and use, their cell phones and other devices into the classroom—BYOT (Bring Your Own Technology), as he calls it. This is a transformative step, as most schools make students either leave their own devices in lockers or turn them off. This helps students to begin to see their smartphones as portals of learning. This allows for four new learning dynamics to occur: global connectivity, anytime/anywhere/any device learning, open source/crowdsourcing, and personalization/choice. In other words, the real world of the Shift Age we prepare our children for. This practice will begin first in the developed countries where smartphones are now in the majority of phones used. In developing countries, cell phones are significantly cheaper than in developed countries. In these poorer countries, schools will bring smart handheld devices into the classroom for students to share.

Dr. Cynthia Elsberry, the Superintendent of the Horry County School System in South Carolina, is now encouraging connectivity in all classrooms and is creating an initiative to help teachers uneasy with technology become comfortable as they interact with their Digital Native students. This initiative will include Digital Native students helping to teach the teachers. This is transformative, as teachers of the Baby Boomer generation are openly acknowledging that in the area of digital expertise, they, the teachers, must learn from their students. All around the world, the Boomer generation is not up to speed with their students in the digital device realm.

> Superintendent Pam Heath, in the small school district of Martinsville, VA, is mobilizing the entire community to realize that the entire community needs to be mobilized to break the economic downward spiral initiated by the loss of the textile industry. Local leaders everywhere must become involved in such transformative processes, as the entire school system has become so full of institutionalized, bureaucratic legacy thinking that transformation needs to be initiated locally, school by school and district by district. This is where the phase transition is occurring: in communities that unite behind the superintendent to initiate local change for local needs, regardless of the national guidelines created by politicians.

I take the time to highlight just a few of these committed education leaders, as the change in K–12 is happening at the local level—"national politics be damned," as some educators like to say—and it is happening fast. A transformation is rapidly taking place, one school at a time, one school district at a time. The technology and connectivity of the world is and will change the classrooms in the next few years. How K–12 education looked in 2012 will seem almost stone age by 2020.

We live in a global, ever-changing world. How can we ask our children to not participate in this world? And yet, we have school buildings that are open less than 25 percent of the time: 8:00 a.m. to 4:00 p.m. and eight months of the year in a world that is 24/7 and always on. We now live in a world where all of the world's knowledge is two to four key strokes away, and we still think it intelligent to ask our children to spend time doing rote memorization? How can standardized tests have any relevance to this reality? All of this is changing, on the ground and around the world, by educators who simply choose to lead the transformation.

One of the key drivers of this accelerating transformation is the nature of the inbound students. The Digital Natives, the first generation of the Shift Age and of the twenty-first century, are simply different. They will have had more digital experience by the time they start the first grade than many of their teachers. How do you teach a middle school student in the classroom in 2015, when she is spending hours a week doing brainwave computer interfacing at home?

By the time the second wave of Digital Natives are in high school, K–12 will be radically different, thanks in part to the reality of how different these children—the "customers" of K–12—really are from prior generations.

The transformational change in K–12 education in the decade from 2012–2022 will surpass the change of the last fifty years in the United States and to varying degrees around the world. Just in time.

# Higher Education

The way to look at the higher education system of colleges and universities is through the lens of history and relative change. Assume a man from 300 years ago has just been awakened after centuries and is being shown the world of 2012. He looks at a car and wonder how it moves. He looks up to see an airplane and is bewildered. He hears the sound coming from a radio and tries to see the person speaking. He is shown a flat-screen television and not only cannot comprehend what it is, but is incapable of understanding the movie that is playing on the screen.

He then is walked into a classroom at a university and immediately says: "Oh, a university classroom!"

Think about that. Think how much change has occurred in the lifetime of the Baby Boomers overall. Then think about how different the university classroom is from when that generation was in university. Not much. Sure, there are laptops, different lighting and furniture, but the fundamental structure, shape, and form are the same.

Higher education is perhaps the institution most steeped in legacy thinking in every society in the world. It stands upon centuries of history and feels that legacy in and of itself is sufficient for self-perpetuation. How many universities proudly tout the year of their founding centuries ago? The current thinking is that being a centuries-old institution is a good thing. But what used to be an asset, being an ivory tower in a society of commerce, is now its largest liability. The economics are unsustainable, the outcomes are questionable, and the insularity and inefficiencies intolerable. The institutional constructs so long in place are in early-stage collapse.

Higher education will undergo transformation between now and 2020. The 500-year-old university model will change more in the next ten years than it has in the last 100.

# Major Shifts in Education
## LOSE THE IVORY TOWER MINDSET

As we have discussed earlier in the book, the speed of change has accelerated to the point where it is environmental. It is no longer one of the dynamics that we must manage—change *is* the environment in which we live. Old methods of teaching old subjects may remain part of most colleges' and universities' curricula, but increasingly the pace of learning will increase, and the need to alter the curriculum is clear. Due to this rate of change, many of the students currently in college will go on to work in industries and careers that do not even exist today. This of course has been the case for decades. There were no college graduates from the 1960s or 1970s who were taught about creating websites with HTML, or graduates of the 1980s who learned about the digital creation of content. Many of the students of today will live and work in a country that is a different one than where they received their higher education. How will the curriculum change to address these realities?

The curriculum is rapidly moving away from the traditional academic verticals of the past and into a much more cross-disciplinary, student-centric model. A good example of this is what President Anthony DiGiorgio has been doing at Winthrop University in South Carolina. When we first met in 2011, President DiGiorgio explained to me that reading my book *The Shift Age* had been one of the triggers that prompted him to reassess the long-term vision for Winthrop as an institution. In an email to me he explained:

> We realized we had to emphasize global learning, encouraging thinking across disciplines, the capacity to work in teams on complex problems, and use technology fluently. In this new age we had to address growing student interest in individualized majors, interdisciplinary studies, sustainability, global studies, digital communications and faster-pace degree attainment.
>
> Most of our faculty use digital content and online discussion options as part of their classes now because that's how Digital Natives learn best. In short, "nimbleness" is a word we use a great deal more than ever before.

Many of these points (interdisciplinary studies, global studies, faster-paced degree attainment, nimbleness, and digital content and online learning) will be fully integrated into higher education in the coming decade.

President DiGiorgio is actively implementing this vision at Winthrop, but he is by no means alone in his efforts. Around the world, other university presidents are drastically updating the old model of higher education, altering and in some cases jettisoning decades-old practices to embrace the wave of transformative change going on today. It has become clear that holding on to what was and what used to be is a competitive liability in a rapidly changing educational landscape. If higher education is to educate and prepare students for their future, it can no longer be based upon outdated models from the past.

## TECHNOLOGY, CONNECTIVITY, AND COSTS

Accelerating Electronic Connectedness is beginning to play a huge role in this change. Laptops are used in most college classes today. Research can be done at lightning speed, as can collaboration with classmates via the Internet. Online courses of all kinds are now becoming mainstream in higher education. The direction of education is toward a "blended learning" model that combines the traditional classroom experience with the online experience to create a new, more integrated approach that reflects what is going on in the world today.

Major universities are now putting hundreds of video courses and lectures online, for free.[1] This raises the first conflict that will lead to a hybrid model in the next few years. The conflict is simple. If anyone anywhere in the world can consume 120–150 credit hours' worth of the best courses of a university online for free—perhaps in a year—what is the value of a four-year cost of $200,000, to take those same courses on the campus of the same university? Is the socialization of the young adult worth the price differential? The socialization and maturation that young people experience at college is of course extremely important. However, it is being called into question when many courses can now be accessed for free. To what extent do parents and students want to go into debt for a four-year socialization process? Is the knowledge gained from the video courses worth nothing? So is this university in the knowledge business or in the housing and socialization business?[2]

These questions will lead to variable levels of college experiences and degrees. For that $200,000, a student can get the degree that the institution has always provided upon graduation. This comes with all the requisite values such a diploma has provided. For a fee that is a fraction—one tenth?—of the cost, another student can matriculate through the entire course catalogue on video to reach the number of credit hours needed for graduation. This will increase the number of graduates and lower the overall costs of higher education. It will greatly expand the reach of any university that faces the future and embraces this model. Financially, it will offer high-margin incremental revenue. The online program will be called, say, a certificate diploma, and will initially be perceived to be of lesser value. Whether the workplace, the market, and employers consider it of lesser value will be determined through time. It might well be that the perception of "brand-name" universities will continue even at this level as the quality of their video and online courses will be deemed superior.

The cost of higher education has dramatically outpaced inflation for decades in the United States and in other countries as well. This means that perhaps the "blended learning" model can be utilized to allow students to graduate from a traditional four-year institution in three years, cutting 25 percent of the cost. Students can gain additional credit by taking online and video courses whenever they want to without the restriction of when classes are scheduled on campus. This can speed up the time to graduation. In addition, many students are not able to take all the courses they want as they fill up quickly. A blended approach— online and in classrooms—will allow students greater access to highly in-demand courses otherwise not available to them. Students, and their parents, will have a choice. In the past they had no choice, just ever increasing costs.

In addition, there will a refocusing on the two-year degree one can get from a community college. Work has become ever less centralized in our digitally connected world, which is reflected in the increase in employers' need for transportable skills in their employees. Things need to be fixed, maintained, and ultimately reused in a sustainable growth world. The two-year institution can provide this type of education. In addition, there will be a progressive replacement of traditional degrees and degree completion with new modalities for certification and the documentation of knowledge and skills attainment. The fourteen-year education will become more respected than it is today, as it will provide students with marketable talents for employment.

## FROM A KNOWLEDGE SOCIETY TO A LEARNING SOCIETY

The university model of the past few centuries was the lifetime model of education. A college would provide a degree for an education that would serve a person for their lifetime. In the Information Age, the need for even higher level degrees was accentuated, as the college degree did not necessarily provide enough skills and knowledge in an increasingly specialized world. This was called the new Knowledge Society. Some have called the Information Age the Knowledge Age.

That is now obsolete. We have moved from the Knowledge Society of the Information Age to the Learning Society of the Shift Age. In this new era, knowledge is acquired; learning is an ongoing process. The rate of change is increasing exponentially, as is the amount of data being created, as are the new careers and occupations. We now live in a world where only lifelong learning will suffice. As my father Cyril O. Houle prophetically wrote in 1972 in *The Design of Education*:

> The idea that education should enrich life throughout its whole duration is not new, but only in this century has it been seriously believed that such a life was possible for most people and perhaps eventually for all mankind. In adult years almost everyone alive would find it possible to realize some of his potential through [lifelong] education.

Education is now a continuous lifelong process in the Shift Age.

## CREATIVITY

Finally we have to look at what is needed in the workplace in the world in the Shift Age. The single most important quality needed is creativity. The word "innovation" is so overused today it has become a cliché, yet continuing innovation is essential if we are to successfully face the unprecedented problems and opportunities of tomorrow. What is innovation other than introducing creativity into the market or workplace? What is most needed in the Shift Age is a highly developed ability to apply creativity across the board of human endeavor. As stated in Chapter Eight, creativity and the ability to think and solve problems creatively are the most important qualities needed in the work and marketplace at large.

Whom did *Fortune* Magazine, the creator of the Fortune 500, name as the CEO of the decade for the first ten years of the twenty-first century? Steve Jobs.[3] As noted earlier, Jobs was not an engineer; he was a designer. Jobs was a college drop-out but a creative visionary, and he built the most valuable company in the world, leading with creativity.

A very oversimplified way of thinking is that the twentieth century, with all the incredible scientific breakthroughs across the sciences, was a left-brain century. The twenty-first century, with the great need for transformative ideas and creative ways to face and solve our global problems, is and will be a right-brain century. The emphasis must be on creativity, as the right brain must join with the left brain to elevate us all with whole-brain thinking.

Since *Sputnik* was launched in 1957, there has been an incredible emphasis on science, technology, engineering, and math, generally referred to as STEM. We now need to counterbalance this fifty-year science emphasis with creativity. All that great STEM thinking is still needed, but now must be better harnessed by creativity and design. Design is and will be ever more important in the Shift Age as we retrofit the twentieth century, make growth sustainable, and look systemically at how to operate Spaceship Earth.

I am currently the Futurist in Residence and Guest Lecturer at the Ringling College of Art + Design in Sarasota, Florida. The reason I chose Ringling is that it is one of the premier four-year creative educational institutions in the world, and as a futurist I wanted to stand squarely with such a highly respected creative institution. Larry Thompson, the visionary President of Ringling, invited me to become Futurist in Residence (that in and of itself is a visionary act!), as he also sees that creativity is central to the future of the workplace, of America, and of humanity.

President Thompson lives this vision of the essential need for a massive and continuing infusion of creativity in business and the world. Speaking about the United States, he said:

> When I see our country's stagnation and economic woes, I cannot help but think that we need a creative revolution that is embraced by business and endorsed by government and educators alike.
>
> We creatively reinvented ourselves as we moved from the agricultural age to the industrial age and again as we moved from the industrial age to the knowledge age. We must take action now and re-imagine ourselves so that we are prepared for the upcoming age forming now.

Dr. Thompson went on to say:

> Traditional thinking is not working. I contend that creative and innovative thinking is one of the most if not the most critical success factors needed for employees and businesses to succeed in the twenty-first century. Need evidence? According to a 2010 IBM study of 1,500 global CEOs, the most desired skill for leaders of the future is creativity.[4]

As I have written in this book, design on all levels will be critical for humanity's success in the Shift Age, the Earth Century, the new energy landscape, and for all of us working both to retrofit the twentieth century and to make Spaceship Earth a sustainable place for the centuries to come. Again, I am in complete agreement with Dr. Thompson in this regard:

> There has probably never been a better time to be an artist or designer than in today's economy. Indeed, if a business is to thrive in our future economy, art and design will play a critical role if not the critical role—Ñin the future of commerce. I want to see an artist or designer have a seat at every board of directors' table in America. That would be refreshing. That would definitely change the game and fuel our economic future.

Dr. Thompson speaks largely from the view of a college president. He is right that there needs to be a greater emphasis on creativity and design at that level, as that is when young people make their first career decisions. However, creativity must be emphasized, cultivated and praised at all levels of education, from pre-school through all levels of higher education. Currently the institutions of education do a better job of stamping out creativity—that STEM legacy of the *Sputnik* time—than they do of fostering it. Time for that to change!

The collapse of legacy thinking discussed in Chapter Seven, will be accelerated by artists and designers who simply think and see things differently. Going forward, is not new and ongoing creative design essential to successfully go down the road to Utopia?

Creativity, in the broadest sense, is the most important quality humanity needs today.

The good news is that most children start off being creative. The Digital Natives are therefore not only the most connected generation ever, they are also the most creative. They are children who can and will combine the connected digital world with innate creativity to change the world. We need them to do so. To help them achieve this, education at all levels must be reshaped to nurture and foster creativity, particularly with this Shift Age generation. They are the future, and it will be important for all humanity for them to be as creative as possible. They represent a generation that will show up and grow up in the world dramatically differently than any prior generation. We must not, as members of older generations, try to stamp out their creativity, but encourage and enable it.

In summary, the field of education at all levels is about to undergo incredible transformation in the Shift Age. Old structures will give way to new ones. New technologies and use of them will flood into educational institutions at all levels. Lifelong learning will become ever more widespread. The Digital Natives, as the students and customers of education going forward, will alter pedagogy.

The structures of education created during the Agricultural and Industrial Ages worked well for those times. The Information Age initiated technological changes with the introduction of computers and connectivity to classrooms and set the stage for the transformation of education in the Shift Age.

As stated in Part Three, the definition of "transformation" is "a change in nature, shape, character, and form." This is an appropriate description for what is about to happen in education in the Shift Age.

# CHAPTER TWENTY

# THE ARTS

A rt, artists, and the arts express the beauty and often the essence of a society, culture, or civilization. In fact, artists are often suggesting where the society or culture is going. The old line about "life imitating art" certainly applies. In the last 125 years, art has certainly done this, whether it was the futurist art movement or the cubists in pre–World War I Europe giving us an early look into the speed and fragmented aspects of twentieth-century life, or the pop art in the early 1960s that was a precursor to the brand-oriented pop culture of the latter part of the twentieth century.

Music and theater have always been of their time as well, reflecting the sound and drama of current society. From the dissonance of jazz in post-World War II time, to the electrified rock and roll of the 1960s, to today's electronic dance music, all speak of their respective times. Music comes into being as an expression of its time and then becomes preserved, as does visual art, in cultural institutions that honor the great works of the past. It is as though art in all forms leads the way and then, embraced by the culture, it moves into its institutional honor and preservation phase. So art is an early signpost of the direction of a culture. Then, when embraced, it becomes of the culture, and finally the culture institutionalizes it and a new wave begins.

So art is before its time when it first enters society, of its time when society embraces it, and honored and preserved by society when its time is past. So what is the future of the arts in the Shift Age?

# A Look Back

As Futurist in Residence and adjunct professor at the Ringling College of Art + Design, I created and taught a senior-level course for the Business of Art and Design major in the fall of 2011 called "The Future of Creativity in the Arts." The fourteen students in this course were some of the brightest and most creative young people I have ever met. Their charge was to see what creativity and the arts would look like in the years ahead. The process I went through with these members of a Shift Age generation helped to shape this chapter.

The first significant step to determine the future of creativity was to take a look back at the history of creativity in the arts from 1200 to 2010 with an emphasis on artistic breakthroughs. Across about 18 feet of white board, we charted that history left to right, dividing it into three sections. The first spanned the years 1200–1800, the second was 1800–2000, and the third was 2000–2030. The vertical axis of the whiteboard represented the significance of the breakthrough on creativity in the arts. So if the breakthrough was of great influence it was placed high up; less so, lower down.

Then, in green we put down artistic innovations, and in red, scientific discoveries, technological inventions, or innovations. An example of green was Giotto's bringing perspective to painting for the first time in the 1200s or Dutch painting creating art for the middle class in the 1600s. An example of red was Gutenberg's inventing the movable-type press in 1454 or the invention of photography in the mid-nineteenth century.

The first thing to report was that there was more green than red in the first section, from 1200 to 1800. In the second section, there was the same amount of both up to 1900. Then from 1900 to 2000 and from 2000 to 2030, red was in clear domination. The obvious conclusion was that, particularly in the last 100 years, technological innovation and scientific inventions have had a greater effect on creativity in the arts than anything coming from the arts themselves.

The second thing to mention was that the section for the 200 years, 1800–2000, had at least twice as many red and green entries as the 600 years, 1200–1800. The section 2000–2030 had as much as the 1200–1800 section did. This points out the acceleration of innovation and change even in the arts in the last few centuries. This of course reflects the acceleration occurring in many areas of society.

# A Look Ahead

So at the end of the semester, we put together a dynamic presentation on the future of creativity in the arts. It is a presentation that has already proved to be prophetic and which I still think is the best forecast on the subject I have seen. Here were the general conclusions:

» Writers will have ever more direct connection to the reader/consumer, and vertical writing comparatives will occur along the lines of what Pandora does now for radio, providing customized recommendations of authors or books.

» Augmented reality glasses will be used to enhance study and interfaces with the arts. One will view a picture and see all the information about that painting: who painted it, when it was painted, and the history of its ownership.

» The markets and the business models for the visual arts will be split between the market for the physical art objects and the market for the digital images of the physical object. This reflects the dual realities of screen and physical as discussed several places elsewhere in this book.

» There will be collaborative interaction between the artist and the audience in all art forms.

» The performing arts will no longer be contained in traditional venues but will break out to anywhere and everywhere.

» Connectivity and social media will allow distant but connected audience members to experience and participate in theater.

» Holography will be fused into standard methods of performance.

» Projections will be everywhere, not just on flat screens.

## THE FUTURE OF THE ARTS IN THE SHIFT AGE:

» The arts will move out beyond their traditional housings

» The arts will be impacted by Accelerating Electronic Connectedness

» The arts will be more of a shared experience between artists and the audiences

» The arts' business models, largely based upon physical reality, will now develop into dual business models, one for physical reality and another for screen reality

# Accelerating Electronic Connectedness and Art

This third fundamental force of the Shift Age is the dominant force at play here. This connectedness will allow all the arts to move beyond their traditional housings. It has also led to the evisceration of the Concept of Place, one of the five contexts of the Shift Age. This is the dominant context for the future of the arts.

One example is that theater performances can be streamed live over the Internet or recorded and watched later in on-demand mode. This will allow the theater to play to potentially much larger audiences around the world. The 1,500-seat theater or the more intimate 200-seat theater can sell thousands of tickets to people who will watch from their homes. This will create much greater revenue potential for the theater. This will obviously create two different experiences and two different pricing models.

Those in the general vicinity of the theater, most likely on a paid subscription program, might pay $100 for a ticket to see and experience the performance live. The distant viewer might pay $5. So the theater can reach more people with every performance. Those that want to experience the physical reality can go to the physical place. Those that cannot travel to or afford to pay the higher price for limited seats in the physical reality can enjoy the same performance for much less on the screen reality.

In both the physical and screen realities, performance art will become much more interactive. The Flow to the Individual has empowered individuals, and social media has greatly amplified the human need to share. Both of these forces will make performance art more interactive. The audience in the theater will become more engaged and actually participate in ways future playwrights will create. The streaming audience can respond as well with the aggregate response of this audience brought into the performance.

This audience interactivity will also occur as the performing arts leaves the traditional theater and concert hall and moves to more public places. The surroundings and the people will be incorporated into the performance. The economic models of symphony orchestras and traditional theater groups, housed in their culture temples, are

Ralph Remington, the Director of Theater and Musical Theater for the National Endowment for the Arts, had some thoughts on this future of the theater in a recent interaction with me:

"In the future there will be many more small 200-seat-sized theaters, perhaps grouped in a multiplex of several theaters, each playing to a different audience or demographic. This will provide intimacy for those wanting a high-touch experience. This has been a difficult economic model but now with the Internet it makes a lot of sense. Live national and international streaming could greatly expand the audience and the revenue. Both the person attending the performance live and the person watching the digital streaming version would probably pay with a subscribership model. This would work especially well with theater festivals in general and new play festivals in particular."

Remington's vision also raises a concept I have spoken about for years, which is that we now live in a high-touch and high-tech world. We are ever more technologically connected, but we still crave the high touch of the physical performance or the physical art creation. Remington's vision of the future of theater satisfies both needs and both audiences. This will play out in all performing arts, not just theater.

no longer a thriving business model without endowments and contributions. Creating extensions both in the screen reality and in expanded, more public places will regenerate the Industrial Age business models that sorely need it, as they are under constant financial constraints because of historical physical limitations.

# New Business Models

The new business model here is obvious: a two-tiered model of higher prices for the in-person, high-touch experience in the physical reality and lower prices in the high-tech streaming or pay-on-demand screen reality. Books, music, and movies already offer both physical and digital experiences; why not the performing arts and visual arts as well?

This business model will also work for the visual arts, which currently is all based in the physical reality. The painter creates a painting and sells it to an individual or creates a numbered series of prints to sell to a larger number of individuals.

The new visual arts model will be similar to the dual model proposed for performing arts. The artist will sell his physical painting to an individual, who will own that painting. However, the artist will keep the digital rights and can create micro-payments for anyone who might want to download the digital image. This way both realities can be served, and the artist keeps some control over his work while the owner of the physical piece of art receives the benefit of the notoriety that amplification on the Internet will bring.

In addition, this can create communities around artists that can preclude having to wait until the work gets to a museum to be discovered by the larger public audience, often after the death of the artist. The art museum has already moved to a more interactive experiential model in recent years and will continue to do so, creating more social events around exhibits. The Art Institute of Chicago is an example of this model. Art museums will begin to commission works from artists directly that will become public displays of art, such as evening showings of projected, multimedia art onto the façade of the museum or the surrounding buildings. These events of course can be streamed on the Internet. In other words, the art museum will open its building both to the local community and to the Internet creating revenue streams for both. The art museum becomes more than just a building that houses physical pieces of art; it becomes an outward-facing interactive cultural center.

Finally, the future of the arts will increasingly become more influenced by technology, connectivity, and computers. In fact, the craft and technique of creating art will to a significant degree be replaced by technology. The artists of the Shift Age generations will be much more likely to learn how to use a computer brush to paint with immediate and incredible complexity than to use an actual brush with oils or watercolors. Again, think about the characteristics of the Shift Age generations, and it is clear that they will view many aspects of the physical reality of the arts very differently.

So, Accelerating Electronic Connectedness, the changing Concept of Place, technology, and the distinct characteristics of the Shift Age generations will be the strongest influences on the arts in the Shift Age.

The merging of art and technology in the Shift Age may well mirror the merging of biology and technology, one of the five major contexts of the Shift Age discussed in Chapter Twelve. Art will become more technology oriented. The arts will gain a wider audience due to connectivity. This may well dramatically increase the number of those who describe themselves as artists and therefore bring about an explosive growth in the creation of all forms of art in the Shift Age.

# CHAPTER TWENTY-ONE
# BRANDS AND MARKETING

Brands and their marketing will change significantly in the Shift Age. A good bit of this change has to do with the fact that the Shift Age is basically coincidental with the beginning of the twenty-first century. The twentieth century was the century of media as we know it. Newspapers reached unprecedented mass, radio reached into the home, movies became mass entertainment, and television changed the world, followed by cable television. Finally, in the last decade of the century, the Internet brought the century and media as we knew it to a transformative close.

Brands and marketing were completely shaped and driven by this media-centric century, as it was media that allowed marketers to create branding through it. Much of the legacy thinking that defined brands and marketing was formed in the last fifty years of the twentieth century. However, in the twenty-first century and now the Shift Age, all of these definitions and axioms are being challenged and destroyed. The Internet has assumed supremacy. It has subsumed many formerly dominant individual media forms from the last century and instead is becoming their connective tissue. It certainly has fundamentally changed consumer behavior, and of course it is to the consumer that brands are marketed.

# Brands through the Ages

We need to take a larger historical step back to look at brands, as much of what is about to happen to them in the Shift Age will in some way be analogous to their earliest stages.

Brands and trademarks predate the modern era and capitalism. They began to appear when long distance commerce began. Initially people exchanged goods locally and therefore tended to have personal connections to the local producer whose business reputation was known and who had an interest in maintaining ongoing trade relationships. When people began to trade long distance, this personal guarantee and reputation was no longer available, and various forms of "marks" were used to help ensure the buyer of the quality and quantity of the goods being sold. Then, sometime around 5,000 years ago in ancient Mesopotamia, with the structured beginning of long-distance trading, elemental brands, or marks, were used to represent the origin of the product or the maker as one whose reputation or quality had been established.[1]

When the Industrial Age began brands took off. Mass production enabled large-scale production of goods, and steam-powered transportation vastly increased the breadth and speed of distribution. This was when still-existing brands such as Bass Ale in 1876 and Coca-Cola 1887 were trademarked, and Quaker Oats was trademarked as the first breakfast cereal in 1895.

Brands really came into their own in the twentieth century, particularly in America. This was when mass markets were created with the aforementioned media, and mass production further drove down production costs, eliminating the local supplier. Brands became large and national and then, later in the century, multinational. Brands were institutional and had institutional authority. They were large, defined categories and were corporate. Ivory was 99 percent pure, Tide was the laundry detergent for the family. The Good Housekeeping seal of approval was a mark of authority and acceptance. This was particularly true when television grew to dominance in the middle part of the century. Brands sponsored entire shows and then moved to the thirty-second commercial, a model still largely in place today.

However, there is disruption that is clearly present with brands as we enter the Shift Age. This is due in large part to the fragmentation of media over the last thirty years. It is much harder for a company to reach the full potential audience for its brand. In addition, with the advent of social media, the institutional power of brands has been greatly diminished. We have moved from a twentieth-century America, and world, that was largely driven by institutional authority to one today that is often driven by personal authority, as in "I'll ask my friends what they think first." This ascendant power of networked friends who seek each other's opinion greatly decreases the almost godlike authority of brand marketers of several decades ago.

The level of brand engagement on a personal level will only increase as we move more into the Shift Age. Brands have always been somewhat aspirational and to a lessening degree that will continue. Brands that are personal and will speak to individuality will increase in value. *Devoted* is not

Through the past few years I have been working with Owen Shapiro, a partner at Leo J. Shapiro & Associates, a well-respected market research firm. He has provided me with insights into how the ideas I first presented in *The Shift Age*, the Three Forces of the Shift Age primarily, have been manifested in consumer behavior, in the effect of personal technology now has on purchasing decisions, and how much institutional authority has moved to personal authority.

Owen and Leo J. Shapiro & Associates recently developed and deployed a brand engagement index that ties in closely with the concepts presented in the first three parts of this book, particularly relative to the Flow to the Individual and Accelerating Electronic Connectedness. These two forces make engagement a key index of brand success and the ability to predict brand success. Simply put, the top two brand index categories are devoted and benefits, and the bottom two of the nine categories are unconnected and frustrated.

Think about these words. *Devoted* and *benefits* are highly personal in a positive way, as is *frustrated* in a negative way. These three speak to the Flow to the Individual and the personalization of branding today. *Unconnected,* of course, is also personal but reflects what a negative that is as our connectedness accelerates. Frustrated, the lowest level of engagement, is deadly when something else is always available 24/7 somewhere.

an aspirational word, it is a word about personal commitment. Successful brands in the Shift Age will be the brands that gain personal devotional commitment.

This leads to how brands will need to be marketed in the Shift Age.

# Marketing

Marketing, as stated earlier, has been around for millennia. However it was only in the last 100 years or so that it moved to the forefront of business. This was due in large part to the explosion of wealth in the twentieth century and the creation, due to national media, of national consumer markets. Again, it was the creation of mass media that allowed marketing to become what it was until the end of the Information Age in the early part of this century.

The power and wealth of large corporations—and smaller ones that got in early on new media—attracted the best and the brightest minds and creative talents. Companies outsourced much of marketing to agencies, particularly in the second half of the twentieth century. Both the company marketing departments and the advertising agencies grew hand in hand with the mass media entities of print, radio, and most of all, television. Looking back from the vantage point of 2012, it all seemed so simple before the Internet and totally simple before cable television.

Aside from the issue of legacy thinking that is no longer valid, the real driver of change in marketing is the disruptive technology of the Internet and how it has largely "disintermediated" the media business.

As students of media and technology know, there is a life cycle of new technologies in media. They are disruptive, then dominant; then they go into decline; and finally they are dormant but still around. Radio became a mass medium and disrupted the cozy world of print by adding sound to sight. Then television came along and disrupted radio and print by adding motion, then cable television added segmented and targeted audiences to a mass medium, and now the Internet is front and center.

The Internet, however, is different from any preceding disruptive media, with the possible exception of Gutenberg's moveable-type press. It is the first media that not only can replace but has already replaced prior media, or at the very least driven consolidation and dramatic change in the business models of prior media. Prior to the Internet, most media had been described and defined by their respective distribution models. Newspapers were sold in newsstands and delivered to the home. Radio came through radios, television through television sets, and magazines on newsstands and in the mail via subscription. High-speed Internet subsumed all of these physical distribution models. High-speed Internet connectivity has put the newspaper business on life support, has ravaged all other print businesses, and is the fastest growing part of the television business.

What is even more interesting is that media entities developed based upon PC and laptop screens are now at risk unless they totally adapt to the dominant screen of the early part of the Shift Age: the mobile device, be it an app phone, a tablet, or some iteration or combination. The media business has always been a content delivery business. That delivery business now resides on our individual devices. As 3G goes to 4G and then to 5G and 6G, there is nothing we will not be able to consume on the device we hold in our hands.

We access these mobile devices anywhere and anytime, whenever we want. It is the "wherever" that is now the driving force for marketing. The ascendant model in 2012 is to reach the consumer wherever she may be. Not only where she is but when she is there. The platform and therefore the marketing message is totally personal, fully integrated into the patterns of the consumer's life. Not the living room, not the car, not the newsstand, not the mail box, not the fixed sign by the road, but right here, right now and only for me.

The explosion of choice that fueled the Flow to the Individual has now largely run its course relative to media, until the next disruptive technology comes along (see Augmented Reality in Chapter Sixteen).

> The user, the consumer, is now completely in control, and it is the marketer who must first acknowledge that reality and then create the previously mentioned devoted relationship with the in-control consumer.

That is why marketing is in such a transition period in these early years of the Shift Age. Old metrics don't work. New ones have yet to take hold. The Bridge Generation is leaving the business, and the Gen Xers are finally getting a chance in the marketing arena but are having trouble letting go of what they have learned, leaving, once again the Shift Age generations to shape marketing for the next twenty years.

## Memes and Conscious Consumerism

Elsewhere in this book I have referred to "memes to movements." This dynamic will apply very strongly to the marketing of brands in the Shift Age. The definition of the word "meme," coined by the great scientist Richard Dawkins at the beginning of the Information Age, is:

> an idea or element of social behavior passed on through generations in a culture, especially by imitation

and

> a cultural item that is transmitted by repetition in a manner analogous to the biological transmission of genes

One of the holy grails of marketing in the Shift Age will be to actually create a meme or memes that will course through society. These memes may not last long, but they will be hugely impactful and influential for a short time with the possibility of permanently altering the image of the brand. Note the second definition on the preceding page. In other words, a brilliant marketing meme will enter the DNA of consumer awareness and the society at large.

So the meme will be a core ingredient in marketing in the Shift Age. When the next evolutionary shift in human consciousness begins, memes will be what marketing becomes.

Finally, there will be the marketing of conscious capitalism and the products that flow from it. Currently in its infancy in these early years, the alignment of a product to something of benefit to humanity or the earth will soon become an essential, fully integrated part of any marketing effort. Consumers have already embraced this in its infancy. In a world of unlimited choice, the ever more powerful consumer will increasingly choose to purchase products that help humanity or the earth in this time of Spaceship Earth consciousness. Again, this relates to both the word *devoted* and to the reality of personal brands. A product will make a statement of one's awareness, commitment, and consciousness.

Welcome to the world of Shift Age brands and marketing. Forget everything you thought to be true. Don't think that the golden years are in the past, as they have just begun. It will be ever more personal. Brands will be about you and who you are.

# CHAPTER TWENTY-TWO

# IP IS THE WEALTH OF THE SHIFT AGE

M odern humanity has been around for approximately 150,000 years. During this time there have been four ages. Each age has had its primary form of wealth creation.

| AGE | CENTER OF WEALTH CREATION |
|---|---|
| Agricultural Age | Land |
| Industrial Age | Production |
| Information Age | Technology |
| Shift Age | Intellectual Property |

Of course all forms of wealth creation listed above are present in the Shift Age. It is just that in this new age the value of Intellectual Property will be ascendant.

## IP in the Information Age

Intellectual property includes patents, trademarks, copyrights, trade secrets, and all forms of human expression in content. Another simple way to think of IP is all intangible or non-physical assets. Recognition of the value created by intellectual property, particularly in business, truly started to lift off in the Information Age. It took off to such an extent that it changed the fundamental notion of how companies are valued. In

1975, at the very beginning of the Information Age, 16.8 percent of the market capitalization of the S&P 500 was attributed to intangible or non-physical assets. By 1995 that number had grown to 68.4 percent. In 2005, just before the start of the Shift Age, it was up to 79.7 percent. The fundamental transformation of our business economy is now complete, as intangibles remain steady at around 80 percent of corporate value. As my friend Jim Malackowski describes it, we have now completed an "intellectual revolution" no less significant than the industrial revolution more than 100 years before.

# IP in the Shift Age

The Shift Age will see the value of IP become even more important to the businesses which create it, as markets develop to transact IP as a product and companies are bought and sold first for their IP rights. Think of some recent businesses that are pure IP: mobile apps, computer software, and touchscreen technologies. In the past four years I have spoken to some 200 groups of CEOs around the world, mostly groups from Vistage International. When I present this concept of IP as the source of wealth in the Shift Age, on many occasions CEOs have interrupted my presentation to comment on the veracity of this concept. Every one of these CEOs reported that they got more money selling their company because of its IP than they ever could have received based upon multiples of revenue or profits. They all confirmed that the strategic purchaser of their company paid for the IP because of their intention to scale up or leverage the value of this asset. This leads me to tell CEOs and companies anywhere in the world to focus on what IP they have. What is your IP, and what might its value be?

In past ages, IP was seen only as defensive legal protection. That of course is still the case. However in the Shift Age, the Accelerating Electronic Connectedness of humanity is creating new wealth creation models of IP monetization, even including the counterintuitive notion of giving IP away. In this new connected age, content can move rapidly and widely, reaching audiences infinitely more quickly than ever before. Opportunities exist in having your content and your IP recognized by the larger market.

> I often use my own experience as a futurist as an example. Seven years ago, I launched my blog www.EvolutionShift.com. Two to three times a week for the first couple of years I researched, wrote, and uploaded columns under the tagline "A Future Look at Today." In other words, I gave my content away to the world. I committed hundreds and hundreds of hours of work to publish my thoughts to the world, all for free. After about a year I had built up a following. This following then started to reach out to me to see if I would attend conferences. Then I was asked to speak to groups and was paid to do so. Then, when my first book, *The Shift Age,* was published, a lot of the content was updated, reorganized content from my blog. So in two short years after I had started to give away my content, my IP, I was earning a living speaking and writing about the future. The blog of freely given IP has now resulted in a full-time occupation as a futurist. The blog of free content has led me, in the last two years, to speak some 200 times in eleven countries on all six inhabited continents.

The interesting thing about Accelerating Electronic Connectedness is that it has "disintermediated" a number of distribution models. This has allowed creators of content to monetize their creative content by providing it directly to the consumer. Musicians and bands often give away two or three songs on the Internet in hopes that will drive customers to the band's website for a direct purchase of the music, middlemen or distributors excluded. Unpublished novelists sell novels as ebooks for $.99 to create large fan markets. Give and receive in the age of connectedness.

# The Future of IP

At the beginning of the Shift Age, Intellectual Property is only just beginning to be released from the depth of corporate vaults around the world. Until recently, the "market" for IP was limited to a meeting of attorneys who would sit across from each other at a conference table and try to set and negotiate the value of a given patent, copyright, or trade secret. Now the market is opening and becoming more structured, liquid, and global.

There are a number of deep-pocketed companies that buy, control, and license IP as a pure business model. There are other technology- or software-related companies that buy IP to create revenue streams from markets they are not in with their core businesses. Corporate revenue streams generated from pure IP licensing are now a huge global business in a rapid rate of growth.

At a time when technology becomes ever more commodified, it is clear that IP is the driver. Just think of the pure IP business that was created for app phones. Before the introduction of the iPhone in 2007, there wasn't even a market for touchscreen applications. Now it is a multibillion-dollar business—a pure IP business and with a low cost point of entry. There are growing markets for every kind of touchscreen mobile device.

One of the visionary leaders in the world of IP is James E. Malackowski, who I mentioned previously. Jim is Founder and CEO of Ocean Tomo and creator of the Intellectual Property Exchange International, essentially the IP version of a Stock Exchange. Jim has spent most of his life in the world of intellectual property, opening the first ever IP appraisal firm in the 1980s to evaluate the IP owned by corporate clients. Jim now runs one of the most sophisticated merchant banking firms focused on all aspects of IP monetization and management. Shortly after meeting Jim, I began to attend public IP auctions that Ocean Tomo put on two or three times a year. Imagine sitting in a high-energy auction room with banks of telephones on one side of the room to field anonymous bids from around the world. Instead of a painting or a car up on a stage for sale, there were patent schematics on large screens that triggered furious multimillion dollar bids from anonymous bidders. These auctions were some of the first efforts to create a liquid and transparent marketplace for IP.

When I want to stimulate my mind about what the future of IP might be, I have a conversation with Jim. In a recent conversation, Jim spoke to me about it:

We are now in the latter half of the third generation of IP market development. The categories of key players have now expanded from IP owners and intermediaries to IP centric investors and risk managers. As capital flows towards IP as an asset class, a host of traditional market mechanisms are developing including consensus valuation approaches, objective ratings, regional financial service centers, and a global IP exchange platform which will allow the primary trading of IP products as well as IP derivatives and risk hedging vehicles.

Even governments are working feverishly to anticipate these market movements, preparing to establish their business centers as anchor points for the global IP market. Such efforts can be seen in a growing number of sovereign wealth funds purchasing patents from around the world, creation of regional patents (e.g., a European patent) and plans to build a globally interconnecting rating platform for patents. In this final effort, expectations are that each individual patent will have a value score similar to a FICO credit score today—a single metric allowing investors to better understand the financial worth of the asset. These scores will be compared against each other with formal exchange rates similar to today's trading between dollars and Euros.

Jim then spoke about the future of IP in the Shift Age:

We have entered the golden age of Intellectual Property. In the next twenty years we will come to know IP as a currency and a building block. Governments will be active participants in using IP as a tool for economic growth as well as a vehicle to tax to sustain commodity tangible–asset programs.

Importantly, by its very nature as an intangible, IP development lends itself to a distributed model of development. We expect that this will empower individuals and crowd-based groups on a global basis to develop their own IP assets as a product in itself for sale or license on the emerging global market platforms. Think of combining Apple's app store with the New York Stock Exchange. Exciting times ahead!

I agree with Jim that we have entered the golden age of Intellectual Property. The Shift Age will be looked back upon as the time when IP came into its own.

## THE FUTURE OF INTELLECTUAL PROPERTY IN THE SHIFT AGE AND TWENTY-FIRST CENTURY

» **IP will be the wealth of the Shift Age.** As land created wealth in the Agricultural Age, control of production created wealth in the Industrial Age, and creating and inventing technology created wealth in the Information Age, IP will be the wealth creation of the Shift Age.

» **The IP market will become liquid and transaction-oriented.** IP is about to move to a much more open marketplace, leaving the "vaults" of companies and coming to open exchanges.

» **The IP market goes global.** Nation-states and boundaries will mean less every year. This will lead to a globalization of IP with emphasis on "speed to a global market."

» **In the post-digital world, giving away IP will help create value for that IP.** A blogger gives away IP and ends up with a book deal or speaking engagements. A band gives away free songs to promote an "album" that it sells direct to fans.

» **IP will increasingly be valued by influence more than control or exclusivity.** In the Shift Age and the twenty-first century, power will increasingly be measured more by influence than control.

Intellectual Property is and will be the way to create wealth in the Shift Age. What IP will you or your company create in the years ahead?

# CHAPTER TWENTY-THREE

# THE ERA OF BIG DATA

The Shift Age ushers in the Era of Big Data. The amount of data, the amount of information that will be created in the Shift Age, will be far greater that all that humanity has created up to now. The Information Age made us all feel the effects of information overload. Everything that the Information Age gave us is a simple platform for the data explosion of the Shift Age.

## The History and Future of Information and Data

The statistics about the explosion of information here in the Shift Age are nothing short of incredible.

From the beginning of modern humanity to the year 2003, humanity created a total of between 3 and 12 exabytes of data, depending upon various estimates. An exabyte is a million terabytes. By the year 2010, humanity was generating 3 exabytes every four days! In 2012, this means that every day humanity is now creating as much information as it created in its first 150,000 years. Wonder why you might feel a bit of information overload?

Some additional reference points to put things in perspective:

» 50 petabytes (50,000 terabytes) equals the entire written works of mankind from the beginning of recorded history, in all languages.
» It is believed that 5 exabytes would be equal to all of the words ever spoken by mankind, if they were written down.

So we are clearly entering into historically unprecedented territory of data and information creation.

In the year 2010, there were 1.8 zettabytes of data created.[1] A zettabyte is a thousand exabytes. Here are my estimates for future data creation:

| YEAR | DATA AMOUNT |
| --- | --- |
| 2015 | 7.5 zettabytes |
| 2020 | 35 zettabytes |
| 2025 | 175 zettabytes |
| 2030 | 750 zettabytes |
| 2035 | 3,000 zettabytes |
| 2040 | 12,000 zettabytes |

These estimates are based upon taking the current rate of dynamic growth that exists now in 2012 and projecting it forward. There is little reason to think that this rate of growth will slow and more reason to think that it might accelerate. Therefore, the numbers above should be considered conservative projections.

These numbers test our credulity. Again, this is why it is often so hard to grasp the future when living in the context of the present. Relative to data creation, we already feel overwhelmed by the amount of information, and then we take a look at what lies ahead and it can be truly hard to fathom. As stated elsewhere in this book, one of the most frequently asked questions from stressed-out audience members in the question-and-answer sessions after my speeches is how to deal with "information overload." Well, the current "overload" is nothing compared to what lies ahead!

A lot of the recent data explosion, of course, is from the explosive growth of the Neurosphere due to the explosion in number of websites, social media, texting, emails, videos, and everything that we all upload and download from the screen reality. We simply have the means, the technology, and the social desires to generate an ever-exploding amount of content and data. In other words, each of us creates more data than our predecessors could ever have created simply due to how we now live and the Accelerating Electronic Connectedness of humanity.

Going forward, much of this data creation will come from the trillions of smart chips embedded in our infrastructure, machines, appliances, and vehicles. These chips generate data twenty-four hours a day and additionally communicate with other chips. Therefore, much of this data explosion is not necessarily readily available for most humans to consume. It does mean, however, that we will be awash in an overwhelming amount of data, allowing us to better understand what is going on moment to moment and in ways that have never existed before.

So how should we look at this new Era of Big Data that has launched in the Shift Age?

# A New Level of Mapping

A simple metaphor is that the Era of Big Data might be considered the third stage of mapping. The first stage, of course, was the mapping of our physical world: the continents and the oceans. The second stage was the mapping of the ways we traversed the land and sea. This third stage of mapping is the mapping of all human and technological activity, our behavior and thoughts.

Another way to say this is that we are entering a time when all sociology and human behavior can be mapped moment to moment. Almost everything going on with humanity can be known as it happens. In a very dynamic way, this makes anthropology and sociology sciences of the present. It will transform every type of business and enterprise, all of which will and must expand their data consumption and analysis exponentially.

This will lead to an entirely new category of professions that are purely data focused and driven. There will be hundreds of thousands if not millions of data workers with deep data analytical skills needed in this decade alone. This will be one of the fastest growing professions of the Shift Age.

Big Data represents the environmental shift in the way we go about understanding the world and making decisions, enabling unprecedented opportunities to innovate. At the 2012 World Economic Forum in Davos-Klosters, Switzerland, Big Data was declared a new class of economic asset, like currency or gold.

The smartest businessman I know regarding this new Era of Big Data is a friend of mine, Ark Rozental. Ark is the Cofounder and Chief Strategist of a company, Reach Smarter, that is completely about leveraging data-driven insights to transform business in the Era of Big Data. Ark and I have had a number of conversations about this topic. His thoughts from a recent exchange are worth sharing.

"The Big Data Era represents a universal challenge of identifying how and what data to use. To survive, organizations will shift priorities to harness this data for patterns and insights that provide opportunities to add value to the bottom line. The best of them will commit their entire organization to the pursuit of data for the sole purpose of elevating the consumer experience at every touch point. The traditional reactive model of analyze and respond, where companies mine historic data to learn how [transactions are] performed, will give way to predictive analytics and proactive action."

Ark went on to say:

"Therefore, getting closer to the individual will be the most important dimension to realize long-term organizational growth strategy in the next five years. We have arrived at a seminal moment in the history of human communication–the point where further vertical acceleration of communication will test limits of human ability to communicate effectively. The point where communication focus will have to shift from speed and volume to a hyper-focused feeding and nurturing of one's augmented reality, times [the] world's population. This will put Big Data at the center of every industry and field for the coming decades."

Ark is correct. It is hard to overstate the significance, the power, and the transformation of business that the Era of Big Data will bring.

# Business and the Era of Big Data

This data explosion, I am sure, will induce both personal and institutional catatonia in many. What can businesses do? What must they do? What will the business of the future do in this era?

Obviously, education will be transformed. In this time, we will move ever more away from teaching facts to developing skills to analyze massive amounts of data in dynamic ways. We are now at a moment of singularity in society. It is less about what you learned than what you are learning.

After conversations with Ark and others, here are some forecasts.

Big Data developments to take place in the next two or three years:

» Data will become the most critical organizational asset and liability
» Protection and privacy of data will be what keeps leaders up at night in every industry and field
» There will be a significant near-term shortage of data-literate workers further fueled by the generational gap between producers of and exploiters of Big Data
» Every screen will get "smart" and will be "connected"
» There will be legislation along the lines of the do-not-call list to protect individuals against targeted data use
» Yesterday's data will start to become tomorrow's action plan

Big Data developments to take place in the next five to twenty years:

» Bioinformatics will finally crack the code of all the protein sequences, structures, functions, pathways, and genetic interactions
» The computing power of "smart" devices will begin approaching that of the human brain
» Entire new fields of endeavor and study will be created. These will flow from the current fields of IT, sociology, anthropology, research, marketing research, and financial forecasting. Predictions will be ever easier to make as trends can now be viewed dynamically, as they occur
» An ever greater sense of our collective whole, our collective unity, will develop as we learn more about what all of us just did today
» Big Data will drive human endeavor as much as it documents it

The Era of Big Data will be one of the most significant developments of the Shift Age.

# CHAPTER TWENTY-FOUR

# SOCIETY AND ECONOMICS

In the Shift Age, society and social conventions and definitions are certainly undergoing great shifts and will continue to do so. Again, an entire book could be written on this topic alone. However, in the last five years of speaking to audiences all over the world, I have noticed several areas of society and human endeavor that are of consistent interest and consistently come up in the question-and-answer session after a speech. It is some of these, not dealt with elsewhere in the book, that we take a look at here.

## Retirement

The social concept of retirement is steeped in legacy thought. The now-fading vision of retirement was created during the post-World War II economic boom in developed countries. The idea of retiring at age sixty-five, or at age sixty if one was vested in a secure pension plan, became a set model. Work until that age, get a gold watch, have a nice retirement party, and walk out of the workplace to move to a sunny place and play golf, shuffleboard, and bridge. Nice! This reality existed when the average lifespan was around seventy, so sixty-five gave us all a few years in the sun.

This was the model for the Great Generation and the Silent Generation. The parents of the Baby Boomer Generation were the last one that could actually embrace this retirement vision en masse.

The majority of the Bridge Generation does not have this as a reality. The tech, real estate, and stock bubbles of the great recession, following decades of living large and in debt, took that off the table. The new reality is no sudden retirement, just working longer or slowly fading away.

Accelerating Electronic Connectedness will change retirement as much as it has changed most other things. It will allow people to add value, create content, and participate, yet still not stand in the full-time work grind they no longer want. In the Shift Age, Intellectual Property —IP—is what will create wealth. Age is not a barrier to thinking or ideas. In the old retirement model, people worked full-time at a place and then retired. Now, people can move into semi-retirement, leave the office, and connect in to any part of the institution from wherever they are. The wisdom of the elders, so valued in ancient societies, can now be a reality due to humanity's connectedness.

Starting with the Bridge Generation onward, the retirement definition of the last fifty years is dead. It will be replaced by people always connected but at levels that decline through time in the final decades of life. There is no longer any "place" to retire to when we are all connected.

# Consumerism

The Shift Age starts out with significant changes already beginning in the area of consumerism and buying patterns. The three emerging trends here are the move from owning to renting, conscious consumerism, and "less is more," or small is better than big.

## FROM OWNING TO RENTING

The great reorganizational recession between the Information Age and the Shift Age that occurred in 2007 and continues into 2012 was the initial catalyst for this trend. In the United States and many countries in Europe, the dream of home ownership has become a nightmare. The decades-long reality of ever-increasing real estate values was shattered. Low- to mid- double-digit declines in residential values throughout Europe and the

United States eviscerated private wealth, and drove people to bankruptcy. Even as this book is being written in 2012, it has been estimated that 25 to 40 percent of homes in these two areas are worth less than the mortgages on them. In addition, the inability to sell has severely limited the mobility of people seeking employment to move to where jobs are, slowing down employment. So, the historically unprecedented loss of wealth, bankruptcies due to this decline, and the inability to sell to move for work has created the beginning of new way of thinking about ownership versus rental. It is so much of a nightmare that it has broken or at least largely damaged that dream going forward. The percentage of the population that will own homes will decline.

With the "no-placeness" created by connectivity, people will move toward ever greater mobility. Mobility means renting, not owning. This rental mind set is also showing up elsewhere. Look at the Zipcar phenomenon. When a young Millennial woman buys an expensive purse, she now no longer thinks she will own it forever—just until she sells it on eBay, creating a "temporary" ownership mentality.

People will obviously still own homes, cars, and everything else in the Shift Age. It is just that the necessity to own is lessening through time. This is connected to the next consumption trend.

## LESS IS MORE

Years ago I described the 2007–2012 recession as the "too much stuff" recession. Millions of us realized that we had stuff we hadn't ever used, hadn't worn, and had not read, watched, or listened to. The delusional debt-driven sense of wealth ended. We realized, in the developed countries, that less is more. Less stuff means more time. Less stuff means more liquidity. Less stuff means more mobility. Less stuff means reallocation of funds to experiences. Less obligations means more freedom.

What we own and what we have will become ever less of who we are in the Shift Age. The "look at me" phenomenon based upon the extravagant display of things will decline in the developed countries. Developing countries will still be going through that cycle well into the 2020s. This will be a source of contrast, and within the realm of the Spaceship Earth discussion a source of conceptual conflict.

The stuff we buy will be long lasting and environmentally sounder than in the past. Sustainable lifestyles will be the model.

## CONSCIOUS CAPITALISM

Creating wealth and the sharing of it. Making money with a social consciousness. Aligning the purchase of anything with some good work. Creating motivations to purchase that speak to one's deeper or higher sense of self.

All of these ideas are now in ascendancy in the world and will continue. The contexts of the Earth Century, retrofitting the twentieth century, and ultimately an evolutionary shift of consciousness are what will drive these trends. The more collaborative and collective mindsets of the Shift Age generations will lead these trends. As they move up the social and economic levels of the world, they will make conscious capitalism the next stage of how to look at economics. The self-absorbed, planet-be-damned growth for growth's sake of the last 200 years of economic expansion, though it will survive to some degree, will be viewed as a stage of capitalism now passed.

Again, this will rapidly grow in developed countries first and then migrate to developing countries by the 2020s.

# Investing and Economics

As a futurist I am always asked about where to invest and where the "market" is going. I always say, and say here, that I am not an economist, nor an investment advisor. I do, though, see some long-term trends in these areas.

> » There will be recessions and extreme volatility in most markets for a good bit of the Transformation Decade, 2010–2020. This is a result of the debt overhang and overleveraging from the prior decade, from the legacy thinking that is falling away in conflict

with the thinking emerging to replace it. Some of the blame for these recessions will be correctly placed at the feet of Industrial Age governments that cannot move quickly and are politically gridlocked. These bureaucratic governments, as discussed earlier, are the slowest moving institutions in developed countries and are therefore no longer able to provide proactive leadership, but are in a state of constant reaction to events. Add in the highly partisan political landscape over the last few years, and the private sector finds that it looks to national governments for direction where there is none.

» There will be extreme volatility in commodities: volatility in pricing in general, and availability of products based upon volatile pricing. This will be due in part to climate change. It will also change national economies. For example, Russia and Canada will become greater agricultural economies. They are the two largest countries geographically, and climate change and global warming will increase the already vast amount of land available to agriculture in both countries over the next few decades. The energy sector will also experience great price volatility as the world moves to a more integrated mix of energy sources.

» The stock markets of the world will stay in high volatility. There are several reasons for this prognosis. Computer trading combined with speed-of-light connectivity will be a dominant force, creating more investing based on timing and momentum and less on long-term value. Individuals will continue to lose the ability to trade as ever greater amounts of capital move in and out quickly with volume at speeds the individual cannot match. There may indeed be new types of capital markets created to replace those that thrived in the twentieth century.

The Transformation Decade will largely be a volatile time for investments as the old models and thinking behind them are still followed with new models and new thinking emerging. There seems to be some evidence that, during transition times between ages, markets largely move sideways due in part to the changing models and thinking. Economics and investments in the 2020s will look a lot different from 2012, with this decade being the transition from old to new. By the 2020s, most of the legacy thinking from the twentieth century will have been recast in this arena. Once that occurs, there may well be less volatile, more long-term trending in the markets. The growing sense of global reorientation and even reorganization of the 2020s may well bring about long-term prosperity as the new economics and markets are recast to this new reality.

# Politics

The major changes in politics that could occur will most likely be due to the influences of the three dominant forces of the Shift Age and the transfer of power from the legacy thinkers to the Shift Age generations. The legacy parties of the post-World War II era around the world will struggle to survive, as they seem to have lost their ways wandering around the legacy landscapes of their past, which no longer relate to current and future realities rushing toward us. Try to think of a dynamic political party that doesn't have its feet firmly planted in its twentieth century legacy.

Politics has existed primarily in the physical reality for most of recorded history. Now that we are increasingly living with the new screen reality the disparity between the view of politics so well entrenched in physical reality and the emerging, connected reality of screen reality is now creating a huge disconnect. The Occupy meme is a case in point. The politicians in the United States took weeks to respond to it initially, and by the time they did it had gone global. The politicians around the world thought it was just a New York, Wall Street–centric demonstration and then found it on their doorsteps. In other words, the screen reality and connectivity accelerate politics and also make it more transparent and available to all. The physically placed, deliberately paced politics of the last century is already noticeably slower than what is going on in the connected world. I forecast that government will inevitably embrace the potential of high-speed connectivity.

As politics moves to a more globally integrated stage in the Shift Age, connectivity and screen reality will reconfigure this new global landscape in ways that create more immediacy, more thought leadership, more innovation, and more integrated ways for all of us to make ever-faster decisions. That chestnut of political wisdom that "all politics is local" will become less true as we move toward thinking globally and have the Concept of Place be in rapid decline.

There will be a developing generational divide in politics. First the Millennial generation and then the Digital Native generation will find more connection in all areas and issues within their generations than with the older generations. This divide will be one of the demarcations between the powers that are holding on to legacy thought and those that see and live in the developing future of the Shift Age. This will be global in scope. The Shift Age generations will simply point to the problems and ineffective solutions and place them at the foot of the older generations who created them. This will be a generation divide perhaps unprecedented in human history.

# Marriage

The importance of the institution of marriage will continue the decline begun in the Information Age in terms of percentage of the populations of developed nations. New definitions of marriage are occurring as a result. Individuals who identify as gay or lesbian now can legally get married in many places. More people spend more of their lives living alone or single. People will continue the current trend of marrying for the first time at older ages. Religion will have less influence on the institution it largely created. The partnership of marriage and religion, which largely served the social and economic realities of humanity up until the twentieth century, will continue to erode.

# Birthrates

The replacement rate for any population is 2.1 children born for every childbearing woman of age. As discussed in Chapter Three, a general global decline in birthrates began with the Shift Age. The bell curve of the explosion of the global population between 1950 and 2050 is on the down slope.

The developed countries of the world are, for the most part, below the 2.1 replacement rate. The developing countries' birthrates, while above that number, are in general decline. As countries become more affluent, more urban, and more medically advanced, birthrates decline. Every year we are now seeing millions of people both moving to cities and entering the middle class for the first time in most developing countries.

The legacy thinking about falling birthrates and therefore aging populations around the world is that this is a bad thing. The reason for this thinking is that more and more older people will be depending upon a shrinking base of younger people. This thinking is certainly valid when looking at some specific towns, states, or nations. This thinking also sits within the larger, no longer sustainable view that unlimited economic growth needs ever more people to sustain unlimited growth.

When seen from a global perspective, however, declining birthrates are an extremely good thing. In this Earth Century, humanity is now the single greatest force and influence on the planet. We are already stressing the planet's ecosystems. We still have great amounts of poverty and starvation in the world. It is clear that we will reach 9 billion humans sometime in the 2040s with the possibility of 10 billion by 2100. I forecast that by the time we do reach 9 billion, the thinking about global population, the then firmly installed thinking about Spaceship Earth, and the realities of the Earth Century will be such that we will never reach the 10 billion number.

If, by 2040, the Spaceship Earth mentality has not initiated a profound change in how we think about our relationship to Earth, then the ultimate cure for overpopulation may well become a human mandate: **procreate once**. Over a generation or two at the most, the population of the planet could be halved if it was mandated that every woman could only procreate once.

The Shift Age, then, is when we will move toward a constant population and view this population as global. As will be discussed in the Mass Migration chapter, we will increasingly move around the planet, moving ever more toward global citizenry, and this global view will alter how we view the human population of the planet.

Finally, the fact that IP is the wealth of the Shift Age, that we are moving toward an evolutionary new level of consciousness, the ongoing move toward urbanization, and the changing Concept of Place all will influence the stabilization of the population.

# Cities and Urbanization

In 2012, humanity crossed the threshold of 50 percent of us now living in cities. Sometime around 2040, that number will be around 70 percent. This will trigger many trends.

> » It will be imperative to retrofit the twentieth century, as most twentieth-century infrastructures are already at the breaking point and will need to be replaced by twenty-first-century infrastructures. This will lead to the fundamental redesign of urban space to reflect the realities of this century. Cities will become smart, with smart chips everywhere to coordinate the flows and rhythms of the city.

> » Birthrates will decline as women have fewer children in urban areas. This has been true for more than a century, as children are no longer looked at as help for the family farm, women tend to work more in urban areas, and the amount of living space is smaller.

> » The "less is more" trend will become accepted reality. The profligate material indulgences of the twentieth century will be largely history. As discussed, this trend flows through the contexts of the Earth Century, Spaceship Earth, and the reduction, via digitization, of the amount of "stuff" we all have.

» Small, energy-efficient living spaces will become the norm. With all the transformation in technology, smaller gadgets with more functionality will eliminate the need for things like bookshelves, home theaters, and large kitchens.

» The automobile as we know it will be largely obsolete in thirty years, as these megacities of the future will have more personal modes of transport to complement new forms of public transport. In 2012 we can already see the beginning of this trend, with cars much smaller and more energy efficient than a decade ago. In addition, cities all around the world are becoming much more bicycle friendly. One person driving a two-ton car for simple transport will become a thing of the past.

» There will be a greater percentage of temporary or rental living spaces as the mass migration of the Shift Age moves people from megacity to megacity with frequency.

Only a few topics were addressed in this chapter. For any socioeconomic topics not in this chapter, always think of the three fundamental forces of the Shift Age. Simply think about any topic and ponder how the Flow to Global may affect it; we have entered the global stage of human evolution. Think how the Flow to the Individual may change what you are thinking about; people are more powerful as individuals than they have ever been before. Perhaps first or most easily, consider how the Accelerating Electronic Connectedness of the planet will affect whatever you are thinking about. Just looking into any future area through these three lenses will offer insight.

# CHAPTER TWENTY-FIVE

# POWER

Throughout human history there has been power. The power of Mother Nature and the Earth. The power of the planets and their force fields. And of course, power as defined and wielded by humans. Now let's take a look at how power will change in the Shift Age.

## Human Power

Human power has many different shapes and shades. People have been born into power, earned power, seized power, and been given power. A few have created subsequent power over others through the ages due to what they wrote or spoke—Socrates, Machiavelli, Thomas Jefferson, Darwin, and Marx are just a few. No matter how much power these people had while alive, they wielded incredible power for millions who came after them due to their thoughts and writings. Others had even larger posthumous power due to the starting of major religions: Jesus, Buddha, Mohammed, and Confucius are just a few examples.

Many people have also embraced the ideas and beliefs of the original figures to gain personal power over others. Stalin appropriated the writings of Marx in his attainment of authority and its brutal implementation over a nation and its people. Popes have wielded great power over the morality and actual lives of people in the name of Jesus. Recently, radical Islamist mullahs have created personal and paramilitary followings in the name of Mohammed.

# Control Power

Generally speaking, the human exercise of power has been one largely of control. Those that have the power control those that don't have it. Those that follow people with power are granted or appropriated power by being anointed followers. I call this type of power Control Power. It might be physical control, thought control, moral control, or political control: all different forms of the manifestation of power.

In the Agricultural Age, power mostly came from bloodlines and from war. In the Industrial Age, power often came from war victories, the creation and oversight of hierarchies, early-stage democracies, and the control of machines and the power of production. In the Information Age, power came from all of these plus technological invention, knowledge, and use of information. In the Shift Age, all of these forces of control and manifestations of power will continue. However, there is a new clear direction in the definition of power as we enter the Shift Age.

# Influence Power

Simply put, power in the Shift Age will move from Control Power to Influence Power.

The three fundamental forces of the Shift Age, the Flow to Global, the Flow to the Individual, and the Accelerating Electronic Connectedness of the planet, all are reorienting power from being about control to being about influence.

> The Flow to Global means that we are moving into the global stage of human evolution. This means we are moving beyond the nation-state as the highest form of identification. Yes, we may still be citizens of a country, but we are also developing the sense of being global citizens. The idea and wherewithal of controlling global humanity is much harder to consider than controlling a country.

The Flow to the Individual is providing all of us with ever more power. The few hundred media companies have become hundreds of millions of bloggers, video producers, and social media participants. Thirty years ago, media companies and governments controlled media and the news. They largely controlled what we consumed. Now, any human with some sort of electronic connection can have their voice or content consumed by any other human. None of us are trying to control; we are trying to influence others.

The Accelerating Electronic Connectedness of the planet is the obvious dominant force altering this power equation. Now that everyone can theoretically reach everyone else, and do so at close to the speed of light, it is both easier for individuals to influence others and harder for any institution or individual to control individuals. Dictatorships and radical religious sects have almost always maintained control in part by censoring or severely restricting outside information. Control Power relies to a significant degree upon the control of information. We saw this back in Chapter Five when discussing how the common denominators of the "Arab Spring" were electronic connectivity and social media.

This global freedom of expression, this ability to connect with anyone in the world, this ability to organize and coordinate groups of people of any size online, has forever changed the power equation. Control Power is rapidly losing a great deal of its former historical power. The most barbaric aspect of Control Power, the use of deadly force on other humans, will flash up as the last vestige of it.

Accelerating Electronic Connectedness, the third force of the Shift Age, is a force that has changed, is changing, and will change the world in all aspects. It is changing the human relationship with power, already lessening the grip of Control Power. The Shift Age will be the age that transitions humanity from a world dominated by Control Power to a world where Influence Power dominates.

If this should not happen, then humanity may well go down the wrong path in the present fork in the road between Utopia and Oblivion.

# Intellectual Property and Influence Power

As discussed in Chapter Twenty-Two, the wealth of the Shift Age is IP, intellectual property. Anyone can create intellectual property. Some types of intellectual property need significant financial investment and, yes, often need to be protected and controlled. However, there are significant examples of how intellectual property created—and given away—can create Influence Power if not Control Power.

As a blogger for seven years, I have consistently given away my intellectual property. I have given away hundreds of columns and thousands of hours of researching, writing, and promoting my blog writings, for free. I was not looking for control; I was hoping for influence. Giving away my IP led to being paid for it, which led to speaking to thousands of people live and thousands of others via online and offline media. Many of these people have told me that I have changed their way of thinking. Though I do not follow up on all those who have said that to me, I know from many with whom I have stayed in touch that this changed thinking led to changed strategies, tactics, and behavior in their lives and the lives they affect. I now have Influence Power that I did not have before giving away my IP.

Think about the earlier discussion of "memes to movements" and the example of Occupy Wall Street. That meme had incredible power and influenced the thinking of tens of millions in a matter of weeks and months. It was a pure example of Influence Power. Nothing could control it. There were base-level effects of control—police tactics, city ordinances, resolutions relative to the use of public spaces—that pushed back, but ultimately Control Power could not stop Influence Power.

Make no mistake, Control Power is and will be still with us. But with the immediacy of the Shift Age, Control Power will become more illusory, more ephemeral, and less absolute. Influence Power is and will be ascendant in the Shift Age.

## Accelerating the Speed and Power of an Idea Whose Time Has Come

By this point in the chapter, many of you may have had that famous quote from Victor Hugo come to mind:

> "All the forces in the world are not so powerful as an idea whose time has come."

Let's think about that for a minute. Hugo lived entirely in the nineteenth century. So when he wrote that quote, he was looking at history that pre-dated universal use of the telegraph, let alone all the subsequent communication technologies that have come along since. This means that all the great ideas he was referring to had only the transport of printed materials or the spoken word to propagate that idea through humanity. This obviously meant that these "ideas whose time has come" took years and decades to move through humanity, and usually only to the small percent of people who could read or who could converse with thinkers and leaders. Yet he still saw the profound influence of an idea that could spread.

Today, in the Shift Age, an idea courses through the Neurosphere in hours and days. So an idea whose time has come now has unprecedented immediacy. Ideas that used to propagate through hundreds then thousands of people over the course of years or even months can now spread to hundreds of millions, if not billions, of people in minutes and hours.

The potential power of an idea therefore, has never been greater in terms of the speed and magnitude of influence. Ideas do not control people, they influence people and thought. True, people can use ideas to control others, but that is infinitely more difficult if those others have access to sources outside those trying to exert control.

So an "idea whose time has come" can now move as a meme.

# The Direction Is Clear

The flow to Influence Power from Control Power is clear. Just think back on all the forces supporting this irresistible force:

> » Place falls away as a concept
> » Women are in ascendency
> » The Shift Age generations are more collaboration- and group-oriented
> » Connectivity and the technological portals to it will keep empowering the individual
> » IP is the wealth of the Shift Age
> » Education and knowledge will become more universal

In the Shift Age, freedom lies not just in power of the people or for the people—it is between the people. People can now have ideas that immediately empower them. Individual empowerment is a significant barrier to Control Power but a huge amplifier to Influence Power.

Control Power will always exist. The human ego, to some degree, operates on Control Power. It leads us to control our sense of self and usually to control others, actively or passively. Separateness is an underlying part of the perception of self. As individual and separate selves, or individual and separate nations or religions, we intuitively and reflexively fall back into the construct of Control Power versus the other self or entity. That said, Influence Power is moving toward dominance in the Shift Age.

Think now of the evolutionary shift in consciousness that is coming in the Shift Age, and you can see that it will lessen the concept of separateness. As an intuitive collective consciousness expands, the power will be ever more in the consciousness itself, which elevates Influence Power.

Future historians and humanity will look back on the Shift Age as the time of transition from the dominance of Control Power to Influence Power.

# CHAPTER TWENTY-SIX

# NATION-STATES?

## The Global Stage of Human Evolution

The global stage of human evolution is now beginning in the Shift Age. We have moved from family to tribe, village to city, city-state to nation-state, and our only remaining boundary for now is planetary. Of course, all of these human groupings will continue to exist, but they are no longer the only categories that define us and, more importantly, they no longer separate us. We are all, at varying speeds, becoming global citizens.

The Flow to Global is the force at play here. This force started with the beginning of the global economy at the end of the Cold War. In the last twenty years, this global economy has fully taken root and completely recast economics in a worldwide orientation. Chapter Three pointed out that economics is usually the first driver of human endeavor and that culture and politics follow closely behind. This means that as of 2012 the word *globalization* is no longer only an economic term—it is the term that describes what will happen to culture and politics and almost all aspects of human society for the next twenty years.

This global stage of human evolution is a big concept, and one that may not be readily apparent to the vast majority of humans alive today. It is very hard to be an American Baby Boomer who grew up in the city where you still live and think of yourself as a global citizen. You are emotionally connected to your family, your neighborhood, your city or suburb, and perhaps the sports teams and cultural institutions in your area. You may leave this primary geographical and cultural orientation to do some international travel. Perhaps you work for a company that is a multinational or work in a field that has a lot of international customers or partners. This means that you are aware of the global economy but might be too place-based to see it, other than its manifestations in a changed local economic landscape.

The leading-edge people who feel they are at least partly global citizens are often people who have traveled extensively around the globe, visit or live in multiple places over time, have constant personal and business interactions with people from many countries, and have constant awareness of multiple time zones. Another category of people who have a sense of being global citizens are those who see the world through the filters of the Earth Century or Spaceship Earth. These people realize that we all have to be crew and work together in that regard. A third grouping are those who sense that a new consciousness, a new dawn of human awareness, is indeed approaching.

I am an American and proud of it. I live in both Chicago and Sarasota and am attached to both places. I vote in Chicago and have an Illinois driver's license. I am concerned about the future of my country. I have spoken on all six inhabited continents in the last two years. I have subscribers to my blog and newsletters from dozens of countries. So I am from one place and I have a place where I live, yet every day I feel ever more a global citizen. I am increasingly aware of moving into the global stage of human evolution. True, we all have legacy thoughts and an increasingly out-of-date sense of "place," but those come from contexts of our past. But the overall direction is clear: Our future is ever more globally oriented.

# The Nation-State

Countries, nations, and empires have existed throughout the last few millennia. Based upon geography, ethnicities, languages, and religions, these larger groupings of humans are the building blocks of human history. However, the nation-state as we know it today was largely formed during the Industrial Age. During this age, the nation-state reached its zenith. This two-hundred-year period is winding down and giving way to the new global age.

This does not mean that the nation-state will go away. It is just that the concept and purpose of it are in a real process of change. As numbers of countries experience the same issues and problems—financial interconnectedness, climate change, environmental degradation, vast amounts of capital flowing around the world at the speed of light, corporations that operate in dozens of countries, scarcity of adequate water and food—commonality becomes clearer through time. Global problems can only be solved by global solutions. No single nation-state or even a number of nation-states can solve global problems by themselves.

Layer on top of this Accelerating Electronic Connectedness, which connects us all regardless of country, and borders become less real and less defined. This new space is ascendant as the rapidly changing Concept of Place lessens in importance. We are becoming citizens more of a space and less of a place. We call it Cyberspace, not Cyberplace. It is the first global space humanity has connectively and collaboratively inhabited. This Neurosphere does not have any nationality. It may have multiple languages, but it has no borders. Anyone anywhere in the world can log into it regardless of nationality, no identity papers needed.

Of course the nation-state will remain in place. It still is the highest political human construct, as least for now. Nation-states will continue for decades. However, a transition is beginning to occur, from a perception that the highest level of problem solving, the highest level of economic oversight, and the highest level of political philosophy is the nation-state, to a perception that perhaps the nation-state is too restricted and constricted to handle global problems.

The United Nations is a noble organization that since its post-World War II founding has sought to be an objective forum to tackle world issues that transcend any single nation-state. It is often called upon to be a peace-keeping organization or a place for debate among nations. It has been placed on a supra-national level and pointed to as the revered place of resolution, particularly in areas of human violence or suffering. It was created with a noble vision in the postwar world as a place for resolution, to help in part to prevent future wars and inter-country conflict.

Unfortunately, that didn't work out too well. The problem is simple: the UN was created at the zenith of the age of the nation-state, so that even the name reflects that: the United Nations. With a Security Council construct that elevates a few countries to a higher level of power than others, it still is a nation-state-driven entity full of nation-state politics. That is why it can never truly lead in a global world and with global problems—because nation-states stand in their own nationalistic positions, particularly in the Security Council. The entire mindset is a collection of nations, not one of the wholeness of global humanity.

The United Nations will remain as an increasingly legacy institution representing the second half of the twentieth century. It will remain until well into the twenty-first century, but increasingly will be a place for the adjudication of economic and trade issues in addition to maintaining its stellar history of humanitarian efforts. Soon, though, new global entities will come into existence that will alter the perception of where leadership for solutions to global problems will be found. As stated earlier, these new global entities will primarily emerge around individual issues, especially climate change and financial interconnectivity. I think that these are the two issues that will first trigger the creation of global agencies with authority to set policy and guide coordinated implementation of globally oriented solutions.

These global agencies will be the first steps to the eventual creation of a Global Council, which will ultimately supplant the United Nations. Each of these will be limited in authority to addressing a single global issue. These will come into existence in the remaining years of the

Transformation Decade and will lead to the larger Global Council in the 2020s, when the need for such an entity will be abundantly clear.

> During this time, the United Nations will transition to being a place for economic and human rights issues between nations and the adjudication of trade treaties and economic interactions.

Nation-states will continue but will become more focused on the national issues of infrastructure, public safety, education, national economics, and the general well-being of the citizenry. In an ever more globally integrated culture, the nation-state will also take on the preservation of national culture, folk culture, and the cultural histories of the countries, aspects of culture that are increasingly on display in museums and the occasional legacy national holidays.

With nation-states turning somewhat more inward, having uploaded authority to the various global councils on global issues, perhaps there could be an opportunity to institute national happiness indexes, something I wrote about years ago. Why is Bhutan the only country with a history of having a national happiness index?[1] That would be a welcome change in the political landscape: politicians campaigning on how they would increase the happiness index of the citizenry rather than attacking each other.

# Forces and Contexts Initiating the Global Stage of Human Evolution

The three forces of the Shift Age all play a part. The Flow to Global is obvious, as it shifts economics, society, and culture to an ever more global orientation. The Flow to the Individual creates more independent and powerful individuals who can choose to define themselves more globally than nationally. The reason they can is the because of the third flow, the Accelerating Electronic Connectedness of the world. This, as mentioned several times, connects us all without limitations of time, distance, or place for the first time in history. To some degree, nations have existed because of a sense of separateness. This is fading fast.

The evisceration of the Concept of Place of course will affect thinking about any place-based entity, be it a city, state, province, or nation.

The Shift Age generations are and will be much more global in their thinking. The Millennials are working and will work toward more integrative solutions to global problems than their parents. Many of this generation grew up playing video games with other members of their generation from other countries around the world. They have spent the majority of their lives living in a global economy. The Digital Natives will have grown with screens, and screens have no boundaries or nationalities. These Digital Natives will be adults in the 2020s after all the change from the Transformation Decade.

> The context of the Earth Century is and will increasingly orient us all to a more global view. In the Anthropocene Era, when humanity is the single most powerful force on the planet, we will inevitably realize that getting through the Earth Century in a sustainable way is all our problem.

Finally, the context of the coming evolutionary shift in human consciousness and awareness is completely free of nation-state concepts and limitations. It will be a change in human consciousness.

In the next chapter, we will look at why the Shift Age will be the age of the greatest migrations in history. When historically unprecedented numbers of people move freely and often around the world, the inevitable effect will be to decrease the power of nationalism.

## A Transition Time

This vision of the decline in the global power of nation-states may be hard for many readers to see or accept. That is understandable. We all have minds and thoughts shaped by the Industrial Age and the last century. We have been raised as citizens of nations. (Americans, in particular, who have lived in the post-World War II world, have a sense of greatness and manifest destiny that has become almost their birthright.) This is the reality we know!

What must be remembered is that this is the Transformation Decade, and the points raised in Part Three are key here. The collapse of legacy thinking in this decade will bring the creative destruction of much that is deemed the current reality today. As this accelerates it will allow humanity to face the problems of the Shift Age and the twenty-first century, making the current decade truly the first decade of twenty-first-century thought. Some of that thought will point us clearly to the direction of ever more global orientation. When we look back at the twentieth century, whatever comes to mind—the "American Century," the "Century of Science," the "Century of World Wars"—began with World War I, 1914–1918, when the map of Europe was formed, the map of the Middle East was formed, the General Theory of Relativity was published, and the Russian Revolutions took place. As we look back at the dominant story arcs of the last 100 years, they all began in the 1910–1920 decade.

> Historians in the year 2100 will indeed look back to the Transformation Decade, 2010–2020, as the time when humanity truly started to think twenty-first-century thought. Part of this twenty-first-century thinking is the ascendance of global thinking over nationalistic thinking.
>
> The sense of separateness and separate manifest national destinies that our still-nationalistic mindsets perpetuate will largely recede in the next fifty years.

# CHAPTER TWENTY-SEVEN

# THE GLOBAL AGE OF MIGRATION

## Unprecedented Migration

The Shift Age will be the greatest age of migration in history. A greater number of humans will migrate at some time of their lives than in any prior age. Some of this will be due to the fact that the human population is larger than ever before. This means that the sheer number of us will be a factor. In addition, the percentage of the total population that will experience short- to long-term migration will increase as well. This reality will ramp up in the Transformation Decade and really take root in the 2020s. Let's look ahead to see why.

The global stage of human evolution mentioned in the last chapter points to all of us developing a greater sense of self in the broader scheme of humanity. We will increasingly see ourselves as global citizens. I do already. I may have places I live, but my extensive travel, constant global connectivity, and thinking as a futurist make me feel that I am indeed a global citizen. In my travels I meet many people who also think of themselves as global citizens. They all have a place or two they can call home, but they think of themselves as "of the world" more than of a specific place. This way of looking at oneself in relationship to the world will increase every day.

The global economy is a primary driver of this way of thinking. I have met Americans who make monthly trips to China for business, and Chinese who do the same in reverse. I know Australians who attend dozens of meeting and conferences a year in the United States, Asia, and Europe. I have met Europeans who come to the United States every other week for business. Of course many of these people are in the upper strata of society or the business world. However, they are certainly not the only ones driving this migration to a global perspective.

People all around the world travel to other countries to work if their country is in deep recession or there are better wages elsewhere. The global reorganizational recession of 2007–2012 uprooted many people who realized that staying in their country was no longer economically viable and went elsewhere. The current economic situation in Europe is a case in point, as many Portuguese have been jobless for so long that they are leaving to go work in Brazil, which has a much more dynamic economy. Yet they are not necessarily moving there permanently. They could always migrate again.

Even when economic times are good, people will still migrate for jobs. We are in a global economy, which means that increasingly we will look globally for employment or contract work. Of course there will continue to be local economies. People have to live, eat, and raise families and, for stability, that occurs in a place. Increasingly, however, people will choose the place they want to live or raise a family and then travel around the world doing work where the work is.

## The Forces at Play

The Flow to the Individual is an increasingly important force here. The dramatic increase in independent contractors, sole practitioners, consultants, and advisors means that a lot of the best talent, certainly a good percentage of the most creative talent, will work anywhere in the world on a contract basis. This is very prevalent today, far more so than before the global economy took off since 1990.

This maps nicely with the reality that much of the work done today is collaborative projects. We live in a highly collaborative world. I believe project management is the dominant management practice today and in the Shift Age, as it will allow high-quality people to be grouped together to work on a project to fruition. Increasingly members of this group will be independent contractors, often from other countries, not employees. A group of people will come together around a project that has both a desired outcome and a deadline. They will work together and then disperse. Some members of the team will move on to the next project, with new members coming in for that project. Management is increasingly project based, and on ever shorter timelines.

We are in a global economy, so that means that we are in a global workplace. People will go work in the world where there are employment opportunities for their skills or expertise. The difference between this reality now and that of the past is that in the past, migration most frequently meant a permanent move, emigrating from one's country to a new country. Now the developing idea is to be on the move, to work in a series of places for a variety of reasons. This is something that can now be done in the Shift Age and not before. Why?

Accelerating Electronic Connectedness is of course a primary enabler of this new migratory flow of people around the world. It allows us to see our loved ones every day via video no matter where we are (assuming a good connection, which is becoming more common). We are in constant communication. The only thing that needs to be factored in is time zones. I often say that a good hotel room with high-speed connectivity is a very productive place. I can communicate via email, chat, or video, I can write, I can work out, I can eat and then go give a speech. No one, except of course the live audience, really cares where I am.

» Complementary to this connectedness is the ever-lower cost of this connectivity. Skype is essentially free computer-to-computer and costs very little to phones and cell phones. There are services that allow one to call from a computer anywhere in the world for around $20 a year as the calls are treated as local calls. I remember speaking with my father when I was young and he was on a trip in

Africa, and another time when he was in Europe several decades ago. I remember that those calls were $30 a minute and arranged by an international operator. So not only is there accelerating connectivity; that connectivity is close to free.

» Another influence to this coming massive wave of temporary migration is the "less is more" trend discussed earlier. We will have less stuff and will continue to have less. We have our content in digital form. We can move our stuff and our technology for a several-month stay working in another country by simply checking an extra bag. I travel with 80 gigs of music, which represents hundreds of albums. I listen to this music with various noise-reduction headphones or earbuds. I usually travel with fifty to seventy-five books, all on my e-reader and app phone. Of course I have a light laptop for writing and work. So a "move" is less of a big deal than it used to be.

The Shift Age Generations are another factor in this growing temporary migration. Both generations have been connected for their adult lives, so they by nature are more global in orientation.

During recent trips to Australia and New Zealand, I met Millennials who were making more money there than they could make in the United States and Europe. Many of them had a long-term view of spending three to ten years working their way around the world. In conversations with Millennials, the common thread was their desire to experience the world, work while doing it, and be global in their viewpoint. They didn't think of themselves as on a vacation, or taking a gap year; they viewed what they were doing as part of a logical life trajectory. For example, my son just completed a year working in New Zealand in the environmental and alternative energy sector. He helped author a report that was widely discussed in Parliament. He said to me that he was able to make more money doing this work than in the United States and that his work had a greater impact, as New Zealand was so much smaller than the United States.

The Digital Natives will be even more integrated into this new world and will consider the entire globe as where they live and work. Their life-long reality of always having interactive screens with which to connect to each other will be the one constant for them, so the generation will have least place-based identity of all. If they travel with their parents, they will of course stay in close contact with their friends at "home" via social media and video, so this will be a reality they know at a young age.

## THE GOLDEN AGE OF AFRICA

The Golden Age of Africa will be part of this mass migration. The Transformation Decade will usher in this new great age for the continent. By the 2020s, Africa will be entering a golden age of economic prosperity. There are several reasons for this.

It is the last continent to fully be integrated into the global economy in a productive way. Historically, as countries became successful as low-cost producers to the world, they gradually elevated their economies to the point that they were no longer low-cost. For example, when I was young, Japan was the primary supplier of inexpensive goods to the United States. Then it was Mexico, then Korea, and more recently China. In each case the success of supplying the world as a low-cost producer created dynamic economies of growing wealth that raised costs in each of those countries. This meant that the low-cost production moved down the food chain of developing countries. What will be the last continent where low-cost production flourishes? Africa in the 2020s.

Africa is the second most populous continent after Asia, so there is an abundance of people living at a subsistence or relatively poor level compared to the rest of the world. These people, and the countries they live in, have not been fully integrated into the global economy. That will change. Sure, the continent has many problems such as lack of infrastructure, lingering tribal conflict, corrupt governments, and inadequate health and education. These problems are and will be addressed in the coming decade in preparation for this new golden age.

Africa has great mineral wealth that is now being developed for the global economy. It has abundant sunshine, so as solar power becomes ever cheaper and battery technology continues to develop, it will be able to develop technology to utilize this renewable and alternative energy and help it grow economically.

This golden age of Africa will greatly affect mass migration in the Shift Age. Many educated native Africans will have a reverse diaspora and move back to the continent to participate in this golden age. Millions of others around the world will move temporarily or permanently to the continent as this ascendant trajectory takes off to participate in explosive growth economies. It will become a magnet for global independent contractors and entrepreneurs.

# Global Mobility

In summary, there will always be the desire for humans to "settle down," to have a place they relate to, or a community they want to be a part of. This is human nature. There will be people who spend their lives in one place, some with a multigenerational relationship to that place. There will always be a sense of origin and of nationality. I am not saying these strong, historically grounded aspects of humanity will go away. However, there will be tens if not hundreds of millions of people who will become much more mobile and migratory for at least a part of their lives than at any other time in history.

The three forces of the Shift Age, the Flow to Global, the Flow to the Individual, and the Accelerating Electronic Connectedness of the world, will drive our new mobility. In addition, the changes in the Concept of Place, living in the Earth Century, and being a crew member on Spaceship Earth will contribute to our seeing ourselves increasingly as global citizens.

We have entered the Shift Age. It is and will be a transformational time to be alive!

# EPILOGUE
# WELCOME TO THE 2030S!

Well, here we are in 2033, three years into this new decade. It is twenty years since the first edition of *Entering the Shift Age* was published. It is interesting to look back at that first edition from this vantage point. It was incredibly accurate on some really big things and yet missed seeing some of those beautiful transformations we have now experienced. The book also missed the unpredictable "Black Swan" events that served as accelerants to the changes it forecast. Sometimes catastrophes can move us forward and upward more quickly than can be anticipated.

We can now look back at the 2010–2020 Transformation Decade and realize what an appropriate name it was. All that legacy thinking and the structures and institutions of the twentieth century that seemed to define human reality at the beginning of that decade literally collapsed as we approached that critical transformational period of 2015–2017. The economic and financial volatility that was the first reaction to all that creative destruction soon gave way to the huge bull market and wealth explosion of 2018–2028.

It was during that ten-year period that the older Shift Age generation, the Millennials, began to firmly establish their generational leadership across the globe. The incredibly innovative ways in which the generation transcended national borders to initiate the new global thinking and culture and to lessen nationalism set the foundation for what we all now accept as global citizenship. Of course now, in 2033, this generation is leading us fully into the global stage of human evolution with new ways of thinking and global integration that was hard to imagine twenty years ago.

As we look back to 2013 from our perch twenty years later, it is hard to believe that men were so in control back then. Looking around at the dominance of women in government, business, and culture today, we see that the change is truly stunning! In just twenty years it feels like the gender history of humanity has been and is being rewritten.

The incredible energy breakthroughs at the end of the Transformation Decade came just in time to prevent the economic collapse that seemed imminent with the legacy dependency on fossil fuels. It took the Millennial generation finally demanding a global systems approach to energy to force us to fully utilize all energy sources in a synergistic way. The success of the atmospheric carbon reduction technologies of the last decade now both give us cleaner air and have stabilized and slowed the global warming that was so destructive to our planet and humanity as we entered the 2020s.

Remember what a big deal it was in parts of Europe and then the United States when the life expectancy at birth first reached 100 years eight years ago? Now much of the world that was born in the Shift Age will live to see the twenty-second century. How commonplace it now is in much of the world to have your tissue-engineered organs waiting for when you need them. That capability was only glimpsed in research labs twenty years ago! The current estimate is that 75 million people have organs that they weren't born with. It truly has been a New Health Age!

As we all move around the globe here in 2033, it is hard to imagine forty years ago when there wasn't a global economy, when people spent entire lives living in a single country! It is also hard to remember that as recently as twenty years ago people had to pay a lot for wireless high-speed connectivity. It is now either free or cheap in every country.

As was predicted in *Entering the Shift Age* twenty years ago, augmented reality initiated a tsunami of change in business, education, and entertainment. We now see it as the logical merging of physical and screen realities discussed for the first time in that book. How could we live without it now?

Finally the evolutionary shift in consciousness predicted in that first edition of *Entering the Shift Age* has turned out to be so much more beautiful and meaningful than could have been imagined. The reality of the collective consciousness and awareness most of us regularly experience seems even greater that the dreams and early visions of it going back a century. It really is becoming an evolution shift even greater than imagined. In and of itself it has altered humanity more than anything else these past twenty years.

How wonderful to be alive now!

# NOTES

## NOTES FOR CHAPTER TWO

1. Houle, David. *The Shift Age*, 2007.

"Tim Berners-Lee, Inventor of the World Wide Web, Knighted by Her Majesty Queen Elizabeth II," http://www.w3.org/2004/07/timbl_knighted.

Gray, Matthew. "Measuring the Growth of the Web." http://www.mit.edu/people/mkgray/growth/.

Gruener, Wolfgang. "Internet Ends 2008 with 186.7 Million Websites." http://www.tgdaily.com/business-and-law-features/40811-internet-ends-2008-with-1867-million-websites.

2. eTForecasts. "Cellular Subscriber Forecast by Country." http://www.etforecasts.com/products/ES_cellular.html.

eTForecasts. "Internet User Forecast by Country." http://www.etforecasts.com/products/ES_intusersv2.htm.

Spencer, Donald D. *The Timetable of Computers: A Chronology of the Most Important People and Events in the History of Computers*. Ormond Beach, FL: Camelot Publishing, 1997.

3. See note 1.

4. eTForecasts. "Worldwide PC Market." http://www.etforecasts.com/products?ES_pcww1203.htm.

Brain, Marshall. "How Microprocessors Work." HowStuffWorks, http://computer.howstuffworks.com/microprocessor.htm.

5. Gromov, Gregory R. "The Roads and Crossroads of Internet History." www.netvalley.com/intvalstat.html.

Odlyzko, Andrew. "Measurements and Mismeasurements and the Dynamics of Data Traffic Growth."

"Growth of Traffic on the Internet." http://www.worldhistorysite.com/internettraffic.html.

Fenix, James L. R. "The National Weather Service Gateway: A History of Communications Technology Evolution." http://www.nws.noaa.gov/tg/histgate.html.

Rumelt, Richard P. "Global Crossing (Condensed)." 2006.

"Next Generation Network: Will the BROCs be Googled Up?"

Kende, Michael. "Overview of Recent Changes in the IP Interconnection Ecosystem." January 2011.

## NOTES FOR CHAPTER FIVE

1. De Argaez, Enrique. "Broadband Usage in USA." http://www.internetworldstats.com/articles/art030.htm.

2. Horrigan, John. "Home Broadband Adoption 2006." http://www.pewinternet.org/Reports/2006/Home-Broadband-Adoption-2006.aspx.

## NOTES FOR CHAPTER TWELVE

1. Fox, Stuart. "J. Craig Venter Institute creates first synthetic life form—CSMonitor.com." *The Christian Science Monitor*—CSMonitor.com. http://www.csmonitor.com/Science/2010/0521/J.-Craig-Venter-Institute-creates-first-synthetic-life-form.

## NOTES FOR CHAPTER FIFTEEN

1. "Statistical Overview of Women in the Workplace." *Catalyst*. http://www.catalyst.org/publication/219/statistical-overview-of-women-in-the-workplace.

2. "National Science Foundation." National Science Foundation—U.S. National Science Foundation (NSF). http://www.nsf.gov/statistics/seind12/c2/c2h.htm.

3. Williams, Alex. "The New Math on Campus." *The New York Times*. http://www.nytimes.com/2010/02/07/fashion/07campus.html?pagewanted=all.

4. "Censorship by Religion." Wikipedia. http://en.wikipedia.org/wiki/Censorship_by_religion.

5. Robinson, Mary. "How Women Lead Differently Than Men Do." Big Think. http://bigthink.com/ideas/24227

## NOTES FOR CHAPTER SIXTEEN

1. Tofel, Kevin. "Uh-oh, PC: Half of Computing Device Sales Are Mobile." GigaOM. http://gigaom.com/mobile/uh-oh-pc-half-of-computing-device-sales-are-mobile/.

2. "Moore's Law." Wikipedia. http://en.wikipedia.org/wiki/Moore's_law

3. Kaku, Michio. "Your Cell Phone Has More Computing Power than NASA circa 1969." Doubleday. http://doubleday.knopfdoubleday.com/2011/03/14/your-cell-phone/.

4. Velazco, Chris. "Google's 'Project Glass' Augmented Reality Glasses Are Real and in Testing." TechCrunch. http://techcrunch.com/2012/04/04/google-project-glas/.

5. "Google driverless car." Wikipedia. http://en.wikipedia.org/wiki/Google_driverless_car.

Taylor, Chris. "Google's Driverless Car Is Now Safer Than the Average Driver." Mashable. http://mashable.com/2012/08/07/google-driverless-cars-safer-than-you/.

6. "The History of Atmospheric Carbon Dioxide on Earth." Planet for Life. http://www.planetforlife.com/co2history/index.html.

## NOTES FOR CHAPTER SEVENTEEN

1. "EIA Reports Increased U.S. Natural Gas Reserves." Americans for Energy Leadership. leadenergy.org/2010/12/eia-reports-increased-u-s-natural-gas-reserves/.

2. "Personal computer." Wikipedia. http://en.wikipedia.org/wiki/Personal_computer.

## NOTES FOR CHAPTER EIGHTEEN

1. Ackerknecht, Erwin Heinz. *A Short History of Medicine.*. Rev. ed. Baltimore: Johns Hopkins University Press, 1982.
2. Houle, David, and Jonathan Fleece. *New Health Age: The Future of Health Care in America*. Naperville: Sourcebooks, 2011.

## NOTES FOR CHAPTER NINETEEN

1. Lewin, Tamar. "Harvard and M.I.T. Offer Free Online Courses." *The New York Times*. http://www.nytimes.com/2012/05/03/education/harvard-and-mit-team-up-to-offer-free-online-courses.html?_r=2.
2. Lindsay, James. "Will MOOCs Revolutionize Higher Education?" *The Water's Edge*. blogs.cfr.org/lindsay/2012/09/20/will-moocs-revolutionize-higher-education/.
3. Elmer-DeWitt, Philip. "Fortune magazine names Apple's Steve Jobs CEO of the decade—Apple 2.0—Fortune Tech." *Fortune Magazine*. http://tech.fortune.cnn.com/2009/11/05/fortune-magazine-names-apples-steve-jobs-ceo-of-the-decade/.
4. Thompson, Larry R. "Fuel for Our Economic Future: Art, Design, and Creativity." *Perspectives*, Fall 2011. http://www.hanekedesign.com/wp-content/uploads/2012/01/RinglingCollege_Perspectives_Fall11-WEB.pdf.

## NOTES FOR CHAPTER TWENTY-ONE

1. Bevan, Andrew. *Cultures of commodity branding*. Walnut Creek, CA: Left Coast Press, 2010.

## NOTES FOR CHAPTER TWENTY-THREE

1. "Zettabyte." Wikipedia. en.wikipedia.org/wiki/Zettabyte.

## NOTES FOR CHAPTER TWENTY-SIX

1. "Broad Measures of Economic Progress." Wikipedia. http://en.wikipedia.org/wiki/Broad_measures_of_economic_prog.

# INDEX

# ACKNOWLEDGMENTS

Thank you:

To my son Christopher, who has taught me much, pointed out where I was behind the curve, and shown me that I am right to place so much faith in the Millennial generation. He is a living example of the emerging global citizen of the Shift Age.

To my stepson Jordan, who is a blend of Digital Native and Millennial and who has therefore shown me how different the Shift Age Generations are from mine and thus provided insight into how they will be different as adults.

To my wife Victoria, who has always been "home" for me as I physically travelled the world and mentally and intuitively lived in the future. Being able to come back to such a wonderful and beautiful home keeps me going.

To all the people who have provided inspiration and wisdom that is included in this book: Jack Myers, Owen Shapiro, Larry Thompson, James Malackowski, Karen Woodward, Eric Williams, Cynthia Elsberry, Pam Heath, Anthony DiGiorgio, Ralph Remington, and Ark Rozental.

To the many people who provided constructive input during the Agile Publishing Model process. I would like to particularly thank Jason Apollo Voss, Bob Klosterman, Ark Rozental and Larry Swenson for challenging, insightful yet kind input.

To Melissa Baron for her great research support.

To all the wonderful people at the Ringling College of Art + Design who have provided a home for this "futurist in residence": Larry Thompson, Doug Chismar, Kathleen List, Christine Meeker-Lange, all the faculty and students, particularly those in the Business of Art and Design program who both support and challenge me.

To Devin Lee Ostertag for her always positive, creative, smart help and support. To the Future Wow! team, led by Sarah Victoria McCauley, that included Devin, Stephanie Rischard, Max Pressman, Evan Glantz, and John Steelman.

To the international Vistage and TEC community, from Rafael Pastor to all the great staff, gifted chairs, and wonderful members. Speaking to Vistage groups over the past few years has made me a much better speaker and a smarter person.

To Mike Shatzkin, an advisor and friend, who has been instrumental in helping this book come to market and is the smartest guy I know about the future of publishing.

Thanks to many old and new friends whose friendship and support for me on this long journey has been most appreciated. In some tangible or intangible way you have influenced the creation of this book: Marilynn Preston, Henry Burnett, Larry Swenson, Jonathan Flcece, Jeff Cobb, Debbie Chinn, Dave Abrahamsen, Steve Mazik, Bruce Damer, Jack Altschuler, Robert Tercek, Harvey Kelber, George Rosenbaum, Jack Myers, David and Annette Fox, Tom and Jan Geniesse, and Jason Apollo Voss.

Finally, to all the visionaries and change agents around the world who understand that change is the only constant in the universe. You are all leading the way and helping the rest of humanity move through the transformative changes upon us.

# ABOUT THE AUTHOR

David Houle is a futurist, thinker, and speaker. Houle spent more than 20 years in media and entertainment. He has worked at NBC, CBS, and was part of the senior executive team that created and launched MTV, Nickelodeon, VH1, and CNN Headline News.

Houle has won a number of awards. He won two Emmys, the prestigious George Foster Peabody award, and the Heartland award for "Hank Aaron: Chasing the Dream." He was also nominated for an Academy Award.

Houle is consistently ranked as one of the top futurists and futurist keynote speakers on the major search engines and in the world today. In 2010–2011 alone he delivered 150+ keynotes on six continents and ten countries. He is often called "the CEOs' Futurist" having spoken to or advised 2,000+ CEOs and business owners in the past four years.

*Entering the Shift Age* is his fourth book. Houle's first book, the influential and highly acclaimed *The Shift Age* was published in 2008. His second book, *Shift Ed: A Call to Action for Transforming K–12 Education* was published in April 2011. His third book, *The New Health Age: the Future of Healthcare and Medicine in America* was published by Sourcebooks in December 2011. *The Shift Age* with a new foreword was also published by Sourcebooks in December 2011.

Houle is a member of the faculty and the futurist in residence at the Ringling College of Art + Design.

Houle, when not on an airplane, lives in Chicago and Sarasota.